Go Go Yoga Kids

Empower Kids for Life Through Yoga

By Sara J. Weis

www.gogoyogakids.com

To my parents for raising me to believe that anything was possible.

And to my children for allowing me time to make it possible.

Finally, to my husband for making it all possible.

Contents

Preface

Three boys. That was the total number of participants for the first kids yoga class I ever taught several years ago. I had just completed my training in children's yoga and was eager to introduce kids to the fun, creativity and benefits of yoga. With my love of kids and yoga already firmly in place, I was sure I could get these three unsuspecting boys on board.

I poured my heart into that first eight-week session. I spent hours researching and creating active yoga themes and games that would get their bodies moving and their interests piqued. We were super heroes, jungle animals, warriors, and Lego enthusiasts. I wrote up informative parent notes for each session so the parents would know our theme and the poses we worked on each week. I included the yoga games we played, illustrations, and tips so they could practice poses at home.

Before each class I would try out my lesson and ideas on my own children. If they weren't available, I would sit by myself on my living room floor and run through the lesson out loud. I really wanted to be prepared, and I truly wanted to help them learn and grow. I wanted to give these boys the best possible introduction to yoga that I could.

At the end of the first eight-week session the boys all signed up for my next session along with an additional twelve kids. This quadrupled my roster! I was ecstatic. I had learned so much that first go-around and was completely hooked on the combination of teaching, yoga, and kids.

Fast forward to present day, after thousands of kids, yoga lessons, and games later, I feel like I truly know what works for introducing and engaging kids through yoga. I am excited to share my accumulation of knowledge so you will be able to empower the kids around you with all the benefits and fun that yoga can provide.

Introduction

Do you love yoga? Enjoy kids? Do you want to make a positive difference in the lives of the children you know?

Go Go Yoga Kids: Empower Kids for Life Through Yoga takes the guesswork out of how to effectively introduce and teach yoga to kids. This resource is a complete and creative guide for introducing kids to yoga through movement, mindfulness, fun, and games. Hundreds of yoga games, lessons, and themed poses are kid tested and ready to use. With this guide you will be on your way to instilling the lifelong benefits of yoga in children!

Before deciding to become trained as a children's yoga instructor, I practiced yoga for several years and was familiar with the class structure and poses. As a teacher who has worked with children the majority of my life, I have accumulated a lot of knowledge about the many qualities and characteristics of all ages of kids. When I combined my knowledge of kids and yoga, I knew that a kids yoga practice would look very different from an adult class. There are similar characteristics such as breath work, yoga poses, and a final resting position, but with kids yoga there is a whole lot of interaction between one another, movement, and creativity sprinkled throughout.

Yoga for kids is intended to be fun and silly at times, but it is also engaging and imaginative. After I saw how much the kids enjoyed and benefitted from the yoga classes I created, I wanted to share my knowledge so others can use this book and easily find success introducing children to yoga.

By introducing kids to yoga, they will learn skills that will help them physically and mentally throughout life. Yoga can easily be incorporated in the home, school, extracurricular activities, camps, and clubs—anywhere there are kids who are ready to learn and have fun.

This resource will provide all the information you need to lead hundreds of successful, completely different and engaging kids yoga exercises, sessions, and classes.

Are you ready to learn, embrace your inner child, and have fun? Let's get to it!

Chapter 1: Empower Kids for Life Through Yoga

Go Go Yoga Kids: Empower Kids for Life Through Yoga is a complete and creative guide for introducing kids to yoga through movement, mindfulness, fun, and games. By introducing yoga to kids you can empower them with skills that will help them physically and mentally throughout life. Yoga can be done in many places besides a yoga studio. It can easily be incorporated in the home, school, extracurricular activities, camps, and clubs—anywhere there are kids who are ready to learn and have fun!

Our world is changing, and kids face different challenges than they have in the past. Often they have commitments outside of school that keep them busy with sports, music, academics, and other activities or organizations. There are many demands on their time and also pressure to be successful. Include quickly changing technology, school, family, friends, and other interests and you have kids who have a lot going on.

Kids are stressed. They may not realize what they are feeling, but most have an intrinsic desire and need to get away, unplug, and be in tune with what their bodies need. Yoga provides an opportunity for mindfulness and the ability to connect authentically with others.

Yoga is a skill that can benefit all kids no matter what activities they are involved in or what their interests or abilities are. *Go Go Yoga Kids* outlines both the advantages of practicing yoga and how to go about teaching it so you can reach children of all ages and skill levels.

When kids come to their first yoga class and I ask them what they know about yoga, there are always a few who immediately sit on their mat cross-legged, place their middle fingers and thumbs together, shut their eyes, and let out a deep, "Ommmmmm." This is how many kids (and adults) view yoga. They see it as a serious meditative process that deeply awakens the inner spirit. I do believe that perception is changing throughout our society, and people are realizing that yoga is so much more. Yes, yoga is mindful and meditative, but it is also active, involved, and encompasses not only the mind, but the whole body.

Go Go Yoga Kids: Empower Kids for Life is written for anyone who wants to help kids reap the benefits that yoga can provide. This includes yoga teachers, classroom teachers, youth leaders, counselors, parents, and any others who are seeking ways to enhance learning and social skills in fun and engaging ways. The games and variations are appropriate for children of all ages and can be used in the yoga studio, home, school, or any extra-curricular activity. Get ready to learn, to be engaged, and to empower the kids around you through yoga.

Top Eight Benefits of Yoga for Kids

Yoga teaches lifelong skills that are beneficial to instill in all growing kids. It is especially beneficial for children to learn at a young age that yoga can help strengthen their bodies as well as their minds. Yoga skills and knowledge can be applied and utilized as kids go about their day-to-day lives. Just by taking a few extra moments, it is easy to get children involved and introduce them to the lasting benefits of yoga.

1. **Increases Flexibility and Strength**

   Picture toddlers with all of their flexibility to bend, squat, and move in all sorts of positions that adults often find themselves unable to do. Children are naturally flexible, but somewhere around the ages of six or seven their flexibility begins to diminish. The good news is that by practicing yoga it helps maintain flexibility.

   Yoga also builds strength as muscles are worked in new ways. One of the many things I love about yoga is that it gives both adults and children the ability to create strength in their own bodies and minds without the use of other equipment. The act of holding a variety of poses and breathing can make anyone feel strong and powerful. Whether a pose is done standing, sitting, or lying down, it has its own benefits and can challenge various muscle groups. Being flexible can also result in fewer and less severe injuries. That is good news for kids involved in sport-related activities and other commitments outside of school.

2. **Improves Balance**

   Similar to flexibility, balance is another skill that decreases as we age. Everything from treading on icy sidewalks in winter to holding a tree pose works to maintain your balance. Balance can be improved with practice and many yoga poses and postures incorporate different elements of balance. Often, your body's balance naturally improves while practicing yoga without you realizing it. This is also true with children. In my experience, as kids balance in yoga poses their self-confidence increases as they feel their bodies grow stronger.

3. **Enhances Concentration and Focus**
   Kids are part of a rapidly changing world. Their young minds are often over stimulated with technology and electronics. This means they are often used to getting immediate feedback from video games, tablets, or phones. This can make it very difficult for them to then actually sit, focus, and complete a task in school or at home. Yoga helps children practice concentration and self-control, which then enhances their focus and awareness.

4. **Practices Being Present and Mindful**
   Today, as many parents and kids rush from activity to activity it can be difficult to be still and appreciate the moment. It doesn't start out like that for kids. Picture preschoolers noticing the shape of a leaf or the color of the sky as they dawdle home from the park. Sadly, many kids become accustomed to a fast paced lifestyle until they do not know any other way.

   There is much benefit to slowing down, unplugging, and being away from it all for a bit. A good kids yoga class can provide that. It begins with settling into the moment and focusing on breathing and the body. Children can then practice engaging poses with games and end with a Savasana or quiet time. The end of class usually becomes the students' favorite part while they lie still and "do nothing." They know they worked their bodies hard, and this is a time to give back, be still, and reap the benefits of strengthening their bodies and increasing mindfulness. Being involved in a yoga class keeps the kids present, aware, and in the moment, which is a valuable skill to practice throughout life.

5. **Boosts Confidence**
   Yoga makes you feel good, which increases confidence. I see this all the time in my kids yoga classes when children are able to master a pose they have been working on or see their flexibility and balance improve. You can literally see them step out of the yoga class standing straighter with more self-assurance. They are also calmer, more poised, and confident in their abilities—not only in the next class, but throughout their daily activities.

6. **Promotes Health and Stress Management**
   Yoga is a physical activity that releases happy endorphins. When you leave a yoga class, you feel good inside and out and you want to maintain that feeling. The twisting, moving, inverting, and holding poses during yoga also improves the digestive system.

   Breathing exercises in yoga help calm and center kids. This gives kids the tools to use when they are feeling overwhelmed, stressed, and anxious in life. Instead of logging more sedentary hours in front of a screen, yoga promotes good health, calmness, and positive active movement.

7. **Builds Positive Peer and Social Interactions**
   Everyone is unique and special in their own way, and we all come from different places and backgrounds. In yoga we talk about how poses look differently from person to person, child or adult. With yoga we celebrate and respect differences as we try new postures and poses. Kids enjoy working with one another in partner and group poses and achieving success together.

   Yoga is also about encouraging one another and promoting acceptance, trust, kindness, and empathy. *Go Go Yoga Kids: Empower Kids for Life Through Yoga* provides many opportunities for you to incorporate those positive interactions so kids can learn and grow together.

8. **Sparks Creativity and Expression**
Yoga kids classes are fun and engaging as children move in and out of games, stories, and songs while learning new poses and practicing as a group. Often, yoga classes for kids are centered on a theme to help them learn about new places and concepts. Yoga also helps kids be free, creative, and express themselves. Not only is this fun, but yoga also encourages kids to use their imaginations, to try new things in a safe environment, and to not take themselves too seriously.

Chapter 2: How to
Plan a Kids Yoga Class

I love making lesson plans for my yoga classes, and I enjoy putting different pieces of a class together. Fun lesson ideas that incorporate yoga are always in the back of my mind as I go throughout my day.

Inspiration comes from a number of places, including from the classes I teach at schools, my own children, my personal yoga practice, volunteer activities, and from my community. I love seeing how different thoughts, ideas, and pieces can fit into one yoga theme. It gives me a thrill as I try out new ideas on my yoga students and see my plan and ideas come to fruition. Rest assured, all of the lessons, games, and ideas have been kid tested and proven.

Have a Plan

It is very important to have a lesson plan in place before teaching a yoga class. Kids thrive on structure and having a plan helps you be intentional and build on previous skills. Children have the desire to learn and try new things. Being organized and prepared helps you take advantage of your limited time with them.

Go Go Yoga Kids: Empower Kids for Life Through Yoga provides a blank lesson plan template so you can create your own lesson plans. Before you do, it is important to have an understanding of why each component of the *Go Go Yoga Kids* lesson plan is important. Chapter 3 breaks down the elements that go into a good yoga lesson. You can then add these ideas to your own lesson plan to make your lesson unique and effective.

Go Go Yoga Kids includes fifteen pre-made themed lesson plans that are ready to use. Have fun with them, but please feel free to change or add to them to make them your own. The more comfortable you are with what you are teaching, the more fun you and your students will have.

This *Go Go Yoga Kids* guide also includes ideas, games, and activities, which can be adapted to a school, daycare, camp or home setting with a few tweaks. Read up and then go have fun creating your own lessons!

Yoga Class Setup and Materials

I like to be prepared, and I always go into a class with my lesson plan and materials in place. I also have fillers if the need arises. I have a yoga bag with all of my materials that I carry to each class. I will not use everything but I am always prepared for any circumstances that may arise.

My Yoga Class Bag Includes:

- Lesson Plan
- Theme related supplies such as books, plastic eggs, playground balls, beach ball, etc.
- Bean bags for balance and games
- Handkerchief for games
- Yoga Pose Cards: My favorites are: *Yoga Pretzels: 50 Fun Yoga Activities for Kids and Grownups* by Tara Guber and Leah Kalish
- Jump Rope for obstacle course
- Portable speaker for music
- Whiteboard and dry erase markers

Yoga Mats:

Do you really need them? Depending on where you are teaching, mats may be provided or kids can bring their own. Another possibility for finding mats could be to contact yoga studios and see if they have any unneeded mats. This is also a good opportunity to talk to the studio about the possibility of offering kids yoga classes.

You can also shop online for inexpensive or discounted yoga mats. At GoGoYogaKids.com there are pointers on how to find inexpensive mats or order a mat roll. The mat roll can be cut into 15-18 kid mats because they do not need to be as long as adult mats. Mat prices vary based on the thickness.

You can also use beach towels as a substitute for mats in preschool classes, outdoor yoga classes, and birthday parties. The important part is to give them kids own space. They thrive on having their own area to move, bend, and play. Having their own space helps give them confidence in practicing their poses. It gives them a perimeter on their space which is wonderful for younger ages or children with special needs.

Class Set-Up for Ages 3-6

At the beginning of class, I have my students remove their shoes and socks and leave them outside the classroom or along the wall. Something about removing the restriction of shoes and socks sets the tone for freedom, creativity, and movement in class.

At the very start of class I like to gather the kids in a circle as I begin class with the Welcome and Breath Work Exercises (Chapter 3). This beginning of class can be done without the yoga mats for the younger ages. Mats can sometimes be distracting for kids while you are setting the tone for your class. They can also interfere with the active movement and games while you are having the kids moving around the room.

For this younger age, I will sometimes save the mats to use during the theme yoga poses, building community, and Savasana (Chapter 3). It becomes more special for the students to showcase the poses they have learned on their yoga mats. This also makes for a more peaceful Savasana as they truly have their own space.

Class Set-Up for Ages 7 and Up

Begin by placing your mat and the students' mats in a circle at the start of class. This helps to generate a community feeling, sets the tone for the yoga class, and gives the students a purpose right from the beginning. Having the mats in a circle naturally allows the children to take turns as they share their names or answer questions during the Welcome (Chapter 3). We will often move our mats around during class for games and inversions and place them against the wall.

A Name Like No Other

Learn your students' names as quickly as you can. Do this in whatever way that works for you. This is something I used to struggle with. I really wanted to learn my students' names quickly, but found it challenging for me since I come into contact with a lot of children throughout the week. The key for me has been to say their name, say it often, and make a connection with their name. A good opportunity to do this is during the Welcome portion of class. Everyone loves hearing their name, and it helps build a community feeling from the start.

Be Ready for the Unexpected

Be energetic and excited for your yoga class to begin. Strive to interact and make a connection with your students right off the bat. Kids can be quick to pick up on adults' feelings and moods so if you are having an off day put it behind you and be happy to see your students. You will already feel better by the time your class begins. Having a playful attitude and child-like spirit will make it so much more fun for you and your students. Be up for anything that comes your way. Your class is not going to go exactly as planned, but that is the beauty of working with kids. Be as prepared as you can, smile, and be ready for fun!

Go Go Yoga Kids Lesson Plan Template

Please use this template to create your own kids yoga lessons. Each component is an important part of the yoga class, and it is important to have an understanding of why it is included. Chapter 3 will provide a breakdown of each part of the lesson to help you understand the significance.

Theme:	
Ages:	
Materials:	
Welcome: (3 minutes)	
Breath Work: (2 minutes)	
Sun Salutation: (3 minutes)	
Active Movement: (5 minutes)	
Theme Poses: (5-10 minutes)	
Game: (10 minutes)	
Partner/Group Challenge Poses: (10 minutes) **OR** **Inversion/Balance:** (10 minutes)	
Community Closing: (2 minutes)	
Stillness and Savasana: (5 minutes)	

Chapter 3: Kids Yoga Lesson Planning

Congratulations on taking the time to read and have an understanding of why each part of a yoga class for kids is important. By following the format in this chapter, everything will fall into place easier for you and your students. A well thought out and organized lesson plan will also create more lasting memories and a better understanding of the lifelong benefits of yoga.

Part 1: Welcome

The Welcome is the first part of class. It only takes a few minutes, but it can also be one of the most important parts of class. This portion helps set the tone for how your class will go and explains what your students will be doing and learning as well as what you expect of them. Kids thrive on structure. I have found the class can proceed more smoothly by keeping the class structure set up the same but changing the activities within the lesson.

Gather the students in a circle and welcome them warmly while having them introduce themselves. This will help you get an overall sense of their moods and abilities. Briefly go over the rules. Three simple but positive rules are enough. State your expectations in a positive format and tell them *how to* behave instead of beginning with "No" or "Don't."

Use something similar to:

1. Listen
2. Be kind
3. Have fun

Ways to Engage Students During the Welcome:

- Share your name and one of your skills.
- What do you already know about yoga?
- Why is yoga good for you?
- What is your favorite thing to do?
- Ask a theme related question such as "Which super hero would you be and why?" or "What is your favorite thing to do in the snow?"

The Welcome does not need to be long, but it is a good opportunity to let the kids know how excited you are that they are there and to introduce them to the theme or format for the class.

Part 2: Breath Work Ideas and Exercises

After the Welcome part of your yoga class, the next portion involves helping your students slow down and become aware of their breath and how their bodies feel. The following paragraphs illustrate why breath is important in yoga as well as fun ways you can help your students become more aware of it.

Most newcomers to yoga think it is only about movement and holding poses, but your breath is equally important. Breathing with purpose during poses lets you hold the position longer and feel stronger while doing them. In addition to this, breathing deeply and consciously helps to strengthen the nervous system, calm anxiety, settle into the class, and be in the moment.

Why Breath Work?

It can be difficult to teach kids to become aware of their breath. They are wiggly, busy, and many times focused on what others are doing. Make breath work exercises applicable to their day-to-day lives by asking them questions that will engage them in the practice such as: "When do you need to use big breaths to calm down?" or "When do you feel anxious?" Possible prompts that children can relate to include before a test in school, when they are nervous before a competition or game, if they are frustrated with their siblings, or just being mindful and in the moment.

When I teach the Breath Work portion of class I touch on why breath is important in yoga and how it helps make you stronger, calmer, and able to hold the poses longer and more easily. This involves the students slowing down and sometimes taking a resting position such as Child's Pose or a seated position with hands resting open on their laps.

Sometimes I have the kids put their hands on their bellies when they are seated or lying down and feel the movement or rising and falling of their breath. Putting their hands in front of their mouths and feeling breath move in and out through their noses is also effective in helping them become aware.

Simple Breath Work Sequence

There are several ways to practice mindful breathing in a yoga class, but the main goal is to make the children aware while slowing down their bodies and noticing their breath. The following is a simple sequence that allows students to become aware of their breath.

1. Find a comfortable seated position with hands resting open on your lap.
2. Sit up tall and close your eyes.
3. Breathe in for a count of five and out for a count of five through your nose.
4. Repeat for five to seven rounds.
5. Open your eyes and see how you feel.

This will be a different experience for many kids. Some will probably fidget, look around, and may even make exaggerated breathing sounds. That is expected and okay! Keep with it and continue to practice with your students. Spending just a few moments slowing down, being mindful, and paying attention to your breath will become easier and easier with practice. Soon kids will be able to use these breath work strategies in other places besides a yoga class.

I have also found that going into Child's Pose with their forehead to that mat is a good way to eliminate craning necks and wandering eyes. It helps keep them focused and centered. Try a new breath work exercise each class and soon kids will understand what they are doing and will develop favorite ones that work for them.

Breath Work Exercises For Ages 3-6

Balloon Breath: Breathe in and out through your nose while your hands hold an imaginary balloon. Act as if the balloon is getting larger as you breathe out.

Shoulder Shrugs: Breathe in and out as you raise and lower your shoulders. This is great to do seated or standing and is an easy quick one to do in school or while in the car.

Elephant Breath: Stand with your feet apart. Clasp your hands in front to make an elephant trunk and bend at the waist. Inhale through your nose as you raise your arms up over your head and lean back. Exhale through your mouth as you swing your arms down and through your legs. Repeat several times.

Snake Breath: Sit tall and take a deep breath through your nose to fill up your entire body. Breathe out slowly and smoothly and make a hissing sound like a snake for as long as you can with your tongue up against the roof of your mouth. Repeat several times.

Rainbow Breath: As you breathe in and out, draw rainbows with your arms above your head.

Zig Zag Breathing: This breath work exercise works well with smaller classes that are comfortable with one another. Students lie in a zigzag fashion with their heads on another's belly. Let them get their giggles out and then for 30 seconds have them be attentive to the rising and falling breath of their classmates.

Darth Vader Breath: Breathe deeply in and out while exhaling strongly and sounding like Darth Vader.

Breathing like Waves: Close your eyes and imagine you are an ocean wave. Alternate the frequency of your breath to become shorter and longer waves as you breathe in and out.

Volcano Breath: Breathe in deeply through your nose and then let it go like an eruption through your open mouth.

Feather Fun: Feathers are great tools to use with breath work. Kids can blow a feather up and down their yoga mats as they try to control their breath to keep their feathers on the mats. Children can also do this while moving across the room on their hands and knees and being "in charge" of keeping track of their feathers as they breathe.

Floating Feather: Take turns with a partner lying down on a yoga mat. The partner lying on the mat tries to keep the feather afloat with their breath.

Breath Work Exercises For Ages 7-11

Children of all ages will enjoy the Breath Work exercises listed above, but as they get older it is beneficial to begin teaching them more of the meaning and purpose of their breath for calming and refocusing situations. I like to explain that your breath is a tool which is always with you and can be used in any circumstance.

Ujjayi Breath: Explain that each movement in a yoga flow will happen on an inhale or exhale. The purpose of Ujjayi breathing is to slow the breath down, send it throughout your body, and prevent the mind from wandering. I tell my students to place the tips of their tongues on the roofs of their mouths and take a deep breath through their noses and then slowly exhale out of their noses. Pay attention to the soft hissing sound that this makes.

Back to Back Partner Breathing: Sit back to back with a partner and synchronize your deep breaths so you are able to feel your partner's inhales and exhales.

Rising and Falling Breath: Lie on your back with your hands resting on your stomach and begin to pay attention to your breath. Count how long it takes to take in a big breath. On the inhale, suck in your belly and take your "belly button to spine." Let your breath continue rising up through your rib cage and out to the sides. Exhale at the top of your lungs so as you release air, your collar bones lower and your ribs contract in and down. Make your exhale longer than your inhale.

Take 5 Breath: This is a great technique to teach kids how they can use their breath anywhere such as at school or in sports and can help them feel calm and focused. Have the children breathe deeply in and out of their noses while counting to five. Do this five times and talk about how you feel.

Part of the Breath Work challenge is helping kids slow down enough to be aware of their breath. Another good way to help with this is to add movement to your Breath Work such as moving through Cat and Cow poses. Kids like to completely exaggerate the movements of the poses with their breath. I encourage that as it really helps them see and feel the difference.

After you have your students focused on their breath, you can begin your Sun Salutations. There are ideas on how to teach this in the following section.

Part 3: Sun Salutations

The Sun Salutation portion of a yoga class follows the Breath Work component. I tell the students that their parents do very similar Sun Salutations in their adult yoga classes. The kids love hearing they are learning and doing similar things as their parents or other adults they know.

I keep the Sun Salutation part relatively similar for each class. Familiarity builds confidence and Sun Salutations help warm up many muscles in your body. Similar to adults, kids like to feel in control and can really utilize their breath during the Sun Salutations if they are already familiar with the flow.

Sun Salutations For Ages 3-6

Keeping it simple at this age is very important. Kids like the motion of raising their arms up as tall as they can to touch the sky and then diving forward over their toes. Encourage them to breathe in and out while doing Sun A and repeat several times. This is a Simple Sun A that I use with the younger ages.

1. Stand tall in Mountain Pose with hands at heart center.
2. Bring your arms above your head to Mountain Pose. Can you reach the ceiling?: BREATHE IN
3. Forward fold over your toes: BREATHE OUT
4. Half lift and place hands below your knee caps: BREATHE IN
5. Forward Fold: BREATHE OUT
6. Rise up to Mountain Pose: BREATHE OUT
7. Repeat 3-5 times. Try to get taller and longer each time.

Sun Salutations For Ages 7-11

As older students become more comfortable with Sun A, it is fun to add to it and incorporate other poses. In the beginning, however, keep it simple. I also give more cues on how to hold their bodies.

1. **Hands at Heart Center**: Stand at the top of your mat with feet together or hip-width apart. Feel your spine lengthen as you

stand up tall. Roll your shoulders away from your ears. Close your eyes and take a few deep breaths in and out through your nose.

2. **Mountain Pose**: On an inhale, sweep your arms up overhead and look up between your hands.
3. **Standing Forward Fold**: On the exhale, lead with your heart and swan dive down, bringing your hands to your mat or shins.
4. **Half Lift**: Inhale and come up onto fingertips, or place hands on your shins (not on the knees). Lengthen the spine and keep your back flat.
5. **Standing Forward Fold**: Exhale and lower into Standing Forward Fold.
6. **Plank Pose**: On the inhale, place your hands onto your mat and step back into Plank Pose. Shoulders will stack directly over your wrists. Keep your gaze on your mat and spread your fingers wide. Tighten your core and think of pulling your belly button to spine. The goal is to make a straight line from your head to your heels.
7. **Downward Facing Dog**: Exhale and send your hips to the sky. You should look like an upside down "V." Spread your fingers wide, turn your biceps in, and press your heels actively towards the mat. Your heels do not need to touch the mat. Keep your gaze looking between your knees. Stay in this position for five breaths.
8. **Moving Forward:** On the inhale, look forward and bend your legs. On the exhale, walk or jump to the top of your mat.
9. **Exhale: Standing Forward Fold**
10. **Inhale into a Half Lift**
11. **Exhale into a Standing Forward Fold**
12. **Chair Pose:** Inhale, raise your arms by your ears or bring hands to heart center.
13. **Exhale into Standing Forward Fold**
14. Repeat 3-5 times while encouraging your students to remember their breath.

At the end of Sun A we talk about how we feel stronger, lighter, and more focused. This exercise is a wonderful way to get their bodies warm and ready for the next Active Movement portion of class.

Part 4: Active Movement Exercises

There is a reason that active movement is near the beginning of a kids yoga class. The kids are excited to be there and after their Breath Work and Sun Salutations, they are ready to move their bodies around the room. Active Movement is the chance to put their energy to good use and let them have some fun while making their bodies strong. The main benefits of active movement are to get hearts pumping, build strength, and get their wiggles out (especially in younger ages) so they are ready to focus on the theme-related poses that follow. I love to utilize music during this portion of class as music will naturally get kids moving.

Active Movement Ideas For Ages 3-6

- **Freeze Dance:** Dance around the room and when the music stops freeze in a pose.
- **Follow the Leader:** Kids love to skip, gallop, hop, jump, and walk backwards around the room as a group. Take turns being the leader.
- **Animal Walks:** Start at one end of the room and practice different animal walks across such as monkey, crab, bear, and frog.
- **Rock and Roll:** Kids can do this on their yoga mats and they love it! Have them rock back and forth with their knees tucked in while hugging their legs.
- **Go Sledding:** This is a favorite exercise and so much fun! Have children sit at the front of their yoga mats with their legs crossed and grab the yoga mat in front of them while rocking forward and back. The older kids enjoy this exercise as well.
- **Mother May I; Simon Says; Head, Shoulders, Knees, and Toes; Red Light, Green Light:** These favorite childhood games can all be played with yoga poses and will get kids moving.

Active Movement Ideas For Ages 7-11

- **Round Robin:** Have each child choose a favorite exercise—jumping jacks, squat jumps, burpees, mountain climbers, pushups, or surfer (Warrior 2 Pose on left and right side with jumping/hang time in between). Once they pick their exercise, go around the circle doing each student's exercise for ten repetitions.
- **Wheelbarrow Races:** Kids love this classic partner activity. It is fun to do and builds incredible arm and core strength.
- **Down Dog Hover:** Hold a Down Dog Pose, then hover your knees to the mat without touching. Extend to Plank Pose, and then find your way back to Down Dog. Repeat several times.
- **Plank Challenge:** I like to have a student model a perfect Plank Pose in the beginning to demonstrate what it looks like to have a straight line from head to foot and a flat back.

This will help ensure that the students will practice a good form during the Plank Challenge. Time them for 15 seconds, 30 seconds, or a minute. Jump in and participate to make it more fun for the students. Tell them to challenge their parents with the pose when they get home. They love it. Make sure they know that squeezing their bodies tight, including their legs and stomachs, will make them feel lighter and able to hold the pose longer. Remind them to breathe!
- **Handstand Kick Ups:** With their hands at the front of the mat, have the students kick up as high as they can. You can also turn this into donkey kicks.
- **Updog to Downdog Flow:** Kids enjoy this transition as they begin to gain confidence with these two fun poses. Have them move between these two poses 5-7 times. They will feel the change in their bodies pretty quickly as they begin to lengthen

their muscles and feel stronger. Plank Pose to Downdog also works well to flow multiple times.

- **Downdog Pushups:** Challenge the students to try 5-10. Discuss which parts of their bodies they could really feel working.

Be creative and have fun! The Active Movement portion of class doesn't need to take long, but kids love it when you jump in and actively participate with them. It is also a great time to discuss how warming up their bodies gives them the ability to hold yoga poses longer and make their bodies stronger.

The next section will introduce yoga poses and how to incorporate a variety of themed poses into your yoga class.

Part 5: Yoga Theme Poses

This is the main part of your yoga class where you can introduce and teach poses and challenge your students in many different ways through the postures. I love introducing kids to new yoga poses, and they also enjoy adding new ones to their repertoire. Your theme-related poses are also a great way to differentiate and accommodate for the varying needs of your class. Illustrations of these yoga poses are found in the following pages.

Select three to five yoga poses to focus on per class. Please refer to the following pages for options of yoga poses. I also strongly encourage you to invest in some yoga pose cards (see Yoga Resources in Chapter 12). These cards are wonderful to use directly with kids because the illustrations are vivid and engaging.

The poses you choose can be theme related (see the Themed Lesson Plans in Chapter 4) or skill related such as balance, partner, core, and inversion poses in Chapter 3. I have found that concentrating on three to five poses per class allows the students to focus, pay more attention to correct form, and achieve success with the poses. They will feel themselves getting stronger, longer, and more flexible as they become more comfortable with the poses.

Introduce the Yoga Poses

I like to introduce the yoga poses by modeling them myself, by having a student demonstrate, or by showing a yoga pose card. While I am guiding the students through the pose I ask questions such as: "What parts of your body are working in this pose?" or "Why is this pose good for your body?" Answers for these questions will vary, but balance, focus, and strength are all benefits that yoga poses provide.

Once the students learn and practice these poses through class games and movement they will better remember them and be able to add them to their yoga repertoire to use as needed. While teaching each of these poses I discuss the benefits that each pose provides.

I reference many yoga poses throughout this book. Please refer to the following pages for yoga pose illustrations. Once the theme-related poses are learned it is then time for the fun yoga games and practice.

Yoga Poses

Warrior 1

Warrior 2

Warrior 3

Updog

Triangle Pose

Tree Pose

Bridge Pose

Prasarita

Sphinx Pose

Locust Pose

Side Crow

Savasana

Reverse Warrior	Rabbit Pose	Prayer Twist
Plow Pose	Plank Pose	Pigeon Pose
Mountain Pose	Lotus Pose	Hero Pose
Legs Up the Wall	Supine Twist	Happy Baby Pose
Half Split Pose	Half Moon Pose	Easy Pose

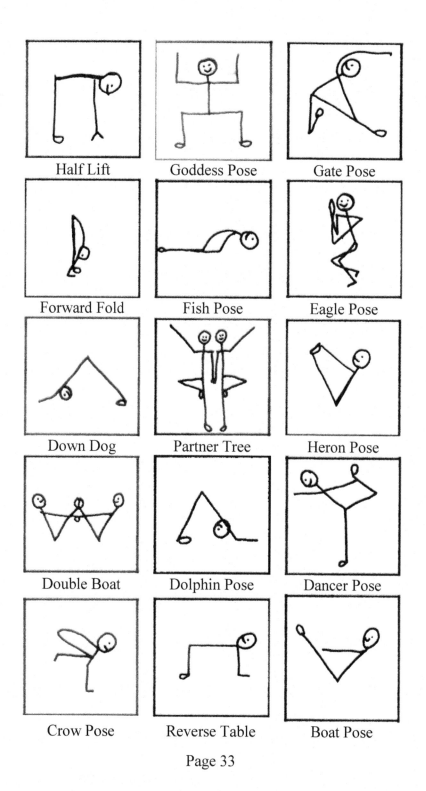

Half Lift   Goddess Pose   Gate Pose

Forward Fold   Fish Pose   Eagle Pose

Down Dog   Partner Tree   Heron Pose

Double Boat   Dolphin Pose   Dancer Pose

Crow Pose   Reverse Table   Boat Pose

 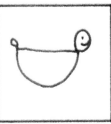

Camel Pose   Bow Pose

Part 6: Yoga Games

Yoga games are a favorite part of class because kids naturally love to play games. Games are also another great way to get kids moving, which is important for growth and health. They help break the ice and allow kids to get to know one another. Games also lead to laughter and provide opportunities to have fun while working together. Yoga games also provide the perfect opportunity to practice poses and develop a deeper understanding of the poses they have learned. Many of these games require few or no materials.

Kid Tested and Proven

I love taking favorite childhood games I played as a kid and recreating them into yoga games. All of the following games have been tested and approved by many willing young yogis from my classes.

These games can be adapted for different age levels by making simple adjustments, and they can be played inside or outside. They can be used during a yoga class, in the school setting, at camps, during other kid-related activities, and at home with your children.

Feel free to adapt and change any yoga game to your setting, age appropriateness, and number of children. The goal of yoga games is to get kids excited about practicing many different yoga poses while they gain strength, improve balance, experience teamwork, and have fun.

Games for Ages 3-6

- **Animal Pick:** Fill a bag with stuffed animals or toys. Have each child pick an animal and make a pose that fits the animal. Do this one at a time so everyone can practice the pose.
- **Drop the Handkerchief** (or something else theme related such as a mitten, pair of sunglasses, etc.): Kids sit in a circle while one child drops the handkerchief or other object behind another one sitting quietly. That child then picks up the object and chases the first child around the circle until returning to their spot. If the child is caught, he or she practices a yoga pose in the center of circle.

- **Freeze Dance:** Play some fun music and let all of the kids dance around the room. When the music stops they must freeze in a favorite yoga pose they have learned. Stay frozen until the music starts up again.
- **Hot Potato:** Pass a ball or theme-related object as quickly as possible around the circle. When the music stops, the child holding the object does a pose and everyone else copies it.
- **Obstacle Course:** This is definitely a favorite among kids, and it really gets them moving around the room. Use whatever objects you have available such as Hula Hoops placed on the ground to do high knees through, jump ropes laid parallel so kids can jump across them like a river, cones to leap over or hop to, or yoga blocks for stepping stones. I like to put all of my "obstacles" in a large circle with a yoga mat and pose cards after each obstacle. The kids move around the obstacle course and perform the yoga poses that are shown on cards. They hold each pose for five breaths or 20 seconds. This is also fun to do to music.
- **Old McDonald:** Find the "Old McDonald Had a Farm" song to play or sing this familiar tune while moving in a circle with one child in the middle (the farmer). The farmer calls out an animal, and everyone tries to do a yoga pose that would match that animal.
- **Pass the Bean Bag:** Children sit in a circle and pass a beanbag while the music plays. When the music stops whoever has the beanbag does a yoga pose with the beanbag. This is a great way to incorporate balance skills such as Tree Pose or Airplane Pose.
- **Red Light, Green Light:** Kids line up at the end of the room while the leader calls out, "Green Light." The kids move across the room but must freeze in a yoga pose when the leader calls, "Red Light." Continue across the room until someone reaches the leader.
- **What time is it, Ms. Yogi?** Similar to the game, What Time is it, Mr. Shark? Students line up on one side of the room and ask,

"What time is it, Ms. (or Mr.) Yogi?" The leader replies a time and a yoga pose. For example, they would need to hold Tree Pose for five seconds for 5 o'clock or 10 seconds for 10 o'clock. When the leader says, "Yogi Time," they must all run back to the start. The first player to reach the leader becomes the next leader.

- **Yoga Flash:** Using yoga pose cards, show a card and see how quickly the kids can copy it. Place the card down in front of the student that makes the pose the quickest. Continue with the next card. A variation is to see who can hold the pose longest or while best utilizing their yoga breath.

- **Yoga Story:** Use a book that has a lot of animals in the story. Do the poses every time an animal is introduced in the story. There are great read aloud book examples in Chapter 12.

- **Yogi Says:** Similar to Simon Says, the leader calls out different actions or yoga poses such as pat your head, jump in place, touch toes, do Down Dog, Tree Pose, etc. The leader chooses to preface the movement with "Yogi says" or not.

- **Yogi Yogi Go**: Similar to Duck, Duck, Goose, students sit in a circle and one child moves around the circle tapping children on the head saying, "Yogi, Yogi" and picks someone by saying, "Go." The first child will jump, hop, gallop, etc., around the circle trying to make it back to his/her seat without getting caught. If caught, they then hold a yoga pose in the middle of the circle.

Games for Ages 7-11

- **Yoga Pet Store:** Put yoga mats in a long line. Each child draws out a card with an animal pose written on it such as cat, dog, bird, frog, and horse. The children then hold the animal pose on their yoga mats. The "customer" walks up and down the aisle to choose which pose or animal they want to buy. The selected child becomes the next customer. Everyone draws a new animal.

- **Parachute Yoga:** There are dozens of yoga ideas that can be done with a parachute. Move it lots of different ways right in the beginning before practicing yoga poses with it because the kids get excited about using it. Shake the parachute as quickly or as slowly as possible. Bring it up as high and as low as you can and walk and shake it in a circle. When it is time to practice the yoga poses call out a child's name and he/she runs into the center of the parachute while it is up and makes a pose. Everyone else tries to guess the pose. The first child to name the pose can go next.
- **Telephone:** This is a great game to use with children that are familiar with the names of different poses. The class sits in a circle while one child chooses a pose and whispers it in a sentence to the child next to them. Continue around the circle with the last child showcasing the pose. For example, "Peter likes to do Pigeon Pose."
- **Pose Challenge:** This is a good game to play when the students are aware of basic yoga poses. Call out two different body parts that should be touching their yoga mat and have them show that pose. For example "Two hands/two feet" could mean the students could show Down Dog, Plank Pose, Cat, Cow, Standing Forward Fold, or a new pose that they invent.
- **Yoga Flow:** Students stand in a circle while one student demonstrates a yoga pose. The rest of the students follow in the circle doing that pose one at a time. Once the pose has made it around the circle the next student makes a new pose and it continues around the circle. If you have students who are beginners in yoga, use your yoga pose cards and let them choose a pose to demonstrate. To keep it simple for the younger ages have the same student select a new pose each time it circles back to them.
- **Follow the Leader:** This is a great way to introduce a Sun A or Sun B flow with the kids in a non-intimidating way. While in a circle, all of the students need to follow the exact movements of the teacher or leader. Make it a challenge by telling them to stay

quiet for three minutes and see how they feel at the end of the allotted time. Play music and make it fun, but be sure to remind them to breathe within poses.

- **Mirror Mirror:** Choose one partner to go first. The partner will slowly move through a sequence of yoga poses while their partner tries to mimic their movements.

- **Person to Person:** This is a fun whole group game to play. Each student finds a partner. When the leader calls out directions such as "back to back" and "head to arm," the pairs of students need to follow those directions quickly. When the leader says "person to person," they must find a new partner.

- **Heads Up Yogis Up:** Similar to Heads Up 7 Up, pick three to seven players based on your group size to come to the front of the room and be "it." Everyone else goes into child's pose and puts their thumbs up. The "it" players each choose one person to push their thumb down. They then return to the center and hold a different yoga pose. The leader calls "Heads Up, Yogis Up." Those children with their thumbs pushed down stand up and hold the same yoga pose as the person that they believe pushed their thumbs down.

- **Opposite Yoga Poses:** Using yoga pose cards, pick a card and try to come up with the opposite of it. For example, Down Dog could be Boat Pose or Frog Pose could be Happy Baby Pose.

- **Pick a Card Any Card:** Students each take a turn to pick a yoga pose card, demonstrate it, and explain how it makes them feel—brave, relaxed, strong. Variation: Have different feelings written on cards such as relaxed, strong, brave, and graceful, and see if the students can think of a yoga pose that would demonstrate that feeling.

- **Shape Maker:** Students sit in two lines with their backs facing you, or in one line for a smaller class. Show a shape to the first two kids in each line. They must then draw it on their partner's back. This continues down the line. The last child in line draws the shape on a piece of paper to see if it matched the original one.

- **Yoga Jenga:** This is another way for the students to learn a lot of poses in one class. Write the names of yoga poses on Jenga blocks and each student takes a turn drawing one out at a time. The student will read aloud the pose and then show it. Continue on around the circle. As per normal Jenga rules, when the blocks fall, the game is over.

- **Body Shapes**: The teacher shows a shape on a whiteboard and students must try to make that shape with their bodies. This can also be done in pairs and small groups. A fun challenge in pairs or groups is to see if they can make the shape while working together silently. Good shapes to use are circles, lines, and certain letters.

- **Museum Guard:** One student is the museum night guard. He or she stands in the middle of the circle. The rest of the students are statues in yoga poses at the museum. When the night guard isn't looking, the statues come alive and move. When the guard turns around and looks the statues freeze again. Whoever the guard catches moving becomes the new guard.

- **Yoga Ball Pass**: Children sit in a circle and pass the ball to the student next to them by only using their feet. No hands! Children may try to lie down, but encourage them to  use their core strength and stay upright like in boat pose.
- **Sea/Shore/Shells:** This is a fun game that allows fun movement while practicing poses that the students have just learned. Have a long jump rope or some other way to divide your room in half. When the leader says, "Sea," everyone jumps to the "sea" side. When the leader says, "Shore," they jump to the other side. When the leader says, "Shells," the students must make a yoga pose. Try going quickly and mix them up. The kids will love it!
- **Yoga Bingo:** This is a great way to learn a variety of yoga poses. Take or make blank bingo cards (these can be found online) and write different poses on the cards. Take turns drawing out a pose, practicing it together, and letting the students mark it on their cards if they have it. The winner gets to demonstrate the poses that created the "Bingo."

This is an extensive list of yoga games, so please do not be overwhelmed. Pick a new one out each class to play with your students. I would suggest spending no longer than ten minutes playing a yoga game. Keep the interest level and excitement high and leave them wanting more. You will then be ready to move on to the Partner Poses and Group Challenges. Ideas on how to teach and lead these are found in the following section.

Part 7: Partner Poses and Group Challenges

Partner poses and working together as a group to accomplish a goal are fun and rewarding. It builds trust and community as well as confidence. Depending on the make-up of the group, I often let the children pick their partners. It is helpful to have someone similar sized for some of the partner poses, but they can definitely be modified.

First, allow the partners a chance to introduce themselves by telling a little bit about what they enjoy and do for fun. Yoga is about building community, so taking time for the children to get to know one another will make working together more fun and memorable.

Safety is a priority in partner poses, and some poses are more advanced than others. Generally, ages five and up can handle the poses with explanation and a demonstration prior. I like to have a pair of students demonstrate each pose before the rest of the class tries it.

These partner and group poses can also be done in a school or home setting. My own family enjoys trying them together, and we modify for all the different ages.

Partner Yoga Poses

- **Seesaw:** This is a great partner exercise for older and younger children or a parent and child to do together. Have each partner sit facing one another on the mat with their feet touching. They will grasp hands. One partner will lean backwards while the other one leans forward over their straight legs. Continue to slowly seesaw back and forth. This exercise is good for working the core and stretching the hamstrings.
- **Double Boat:** This partner pose looks absolutely stunning and impressive when done correctly. Have each partner sit facing each other with knees bent and toes touching. While holding hands, they lift their legs. To help with

balance, the bottoms of their feet should be touching. Then the partners, if able, straighten their legs and lean back slightly as if in a "V" shape.

- **Roof Tops:** Kids love this partner pose, and it could even be done with a group of three. The Roof Top Pose needs to be modeled before the students attempt it. Go slowly and stress the importance of relying on one another and moving  slowly. Partners face one another arm's length apart. They then touch their palms together and press. Each partner takes a small step backward. They should keep taking small steps back until they reach a mutual point. Partners then raise hands up together to form a roof. The third student can then move into Chair Pose between their hands. If the group is willing, try making a larger house with all three people standing and pressing their palms together.

- **Lounge Chair:** One partner is seated and leans forward to touch their toes. The other partner sits directly behind them with legs straight out in front and leans back onto their partner with arms overhead.

- **Double Cobra:** Each pair goes into Cobra Pose facing one another. They should then lift their heads and connect their arms at the top. This is a beautiful partner pose and wonderful for building back strength.

- **Open Heart:** Each child should stand behind a partner with one foot back, one foot forward, and knees slightly bent, holding their partner's wrist. One partner then leans forward and shines his or her heart forward while the other partner helps support them.

- **Elevator:** Partners sit back to back on the floor and hook elbows. They should bend their legs, press into each other's backs, and rise up. See if they can go back down and rise up again as if in an elevator.

- **Double Chair**: This is similar to Elevator, but reversed. Partners stand facing one another and hold one another's wrists. They should be instructed to lean back so they are each supporting one another. Partners then bend knees until they are parallel to the floor.

- **Fountain:** This is an excellent pose to talk about open hearts and partner trust. Partners stand facing one another about a foot apart. They grab onto one another's wrists and lean their heads back so they are looking at the ceiling.

- **Double Down Dog:** This is definitely a favorite pose and one to work up to or save for last. One partner goes into Down Dog. The other partner stands in front of them and goes into Down Dog. The front partner places one foot on their partner's lower back and slowly brings their other foot up to meet it. Younger students will need assistance with this. If the partners are comfortable in this pose have them switch positions.

- **Raindrop:** Each partner lies on their back with their heads touching. With their arms at their sides, they raise their feet above their heads to touch to make a giant raindrop.

- **Plank Walks:** This is a great pose for building core strength and for partners to encourage one another. One partner goes into plank pose. The other stands behind his or her partner and goes into a low squat and gently picks up one foot at a time. This is great for the plank partner to work on balance. Have the partners switch positions.

Group Yoga Poses

- **Group Tree:** Have students stand in a circle and go into tree pose. They can then put their palms together so they are supporting one another. Make the trees as strong as possible by closing one eye and then both eyes.

Can the tree sway in the "breeze" and not fall? Discuss how we are better when we all work together!

- **Happy Yoga Circle:** Students sit in a close circle with their legs straight out in front of them. Have them hold hands with those sitting on either side of them and slowly lean back so they are supporting one another.
- **Hula Hoop Pass:** Pass the Hula Hoop around your body while holding hands in a circle. Do not let go of hands.
- **Human Knot:** Students stand in a circle and hold two hands across the circle from them. Try to untangle the group without letting go of hands.
- **Body Shapes:** With a marker board, draw a shape—circle and triangle work well—or a letter. Have the students try to make that shape with their bodies. Then have the children try it in groups of two or three and finally a large group challenge. I like to change this up once in a while and see if they can make their body shapes without saying a word. This is a lot more challenging than you would think.
- **Down Dog Train:** Everyone in the group is part of train.
- **Down Dog Tunnel:** Kids love making a Down Dog tunnel in a line. Take turns letting them crawl through.

In addition to these ideas almost any balance pose can also be done as partners or in a group. Partner balance poses include Double Tree, Airplane Duo, and Double Triangles with their heads facing one another. More information on balance poses can be found in the following pages.

Have fun with these partner poses and try something new. See if the children can come up with their own partner or group challenge. I am willing to believe that they can! Accomplishing these poses and challenges with others builds teamwork, cooperation, trust, and  confidence, and it creates an overall positive feeling that lasts in and out of yoga class.

Part 8: Balance and Inversion Ideas

Balance

Kids love to work on balance in yoga class because it is fun and challenging. They often don't realize that they are acquiring a skill that improves each time they practice.

Balance poses in yoga improve coordination, increase strength, and develop stability. Balance, unfortunately, is something that decreases as we age unless we continue to work on it. Introducing kids at an early age to fun balance poses is a great way to help them maintain good balance skills.

Each yoga balance pose works to strengthen different muscles and joints of the body. Standing balance poses such as Tree Pose or Airplane Pose strengthen the legs and knee joints. Arm poses such as Crow Pose or Side Plank strengthen the wrists, arm, and shoulder muscles. For this reason, include a variety of balance poses in your classes so students gain the most benefits. In my experience, students get great satisfaction when they master the art of balance.

Favorite Balance Poses:

Tree Pose

Warrior 3
(Airplane)

Eagle Pose

Spinal Balance

Dancer Pose

Extended Hand to
Toe Pose

Arrow Pose

Crow Pose

A few additional balance poses to try are Side Plank, Duck Pose, and Double Toe Hold. Encourage the children to keep working on these balance poses. They will not look perfect every time, but the confidence you are instilling in them will help them to continue to keep trying and have fun.

Balance Tips:

Have your students find a spot on the ground and focus on that spot. You will need to remind them not to watch others, because if they are moving, it will be more difficult for them to hold their balance pose. Success with balance poses takes practice, but they are bettering their skills each time they give it a try. Remind them to breathe as it helps hold the pose and gives them something to focus on.

Using Bean Bags, Blocks, and Mats for Balance Practice:

Bean Bag Balance: There are many activities you can do with bean bags to make practicing balance fun. Have students line up on one end of the room and try to walk to the other side with a beanbag on their head. Then have them try to balance it on their shoulders or elbows. Which other body parts can they think of to use while trying to balance a beanbag?

Next practice stationary balance poses with the kids putting the bean bags on their heads while trying the following poses: Tree Pose, Airplane Pose, Dancer Pose, and One-Legged Mountain. See if the students can come up with their own unique balance poses.

Block Balance: Kids love using any props or materials in class, and utilizing yoga blocks is no exception. If you have access to yoga blocks, they make balance practice all the more fun and challenging. Have them stand on the wide part of the block and begin by lifting a leg and raising their arms above their heads for One Legged Mountain. Next they can try Tree Pose and Warrior 3 while balancing on their blocks. Remind the students to use the yoga blocks safely and appropriately to avoid twisting any ankles.

Owl Pose and Perch: Owl Pose with a yoga mat is definitely a favorite balance pose. Have the students begin at the back of their mats and gently roll it up. This becomes the branch for the owl. Next the students can stand on their mats, balance, and slowly bend their legs so they become owls perching on a branch. I like to have my students bring their hands to heart center or they may want to create wings with their arms. Finally they can slowly turn their heads from side to side as if they are owls.

Inversions

What is an Inversion?

Time to get upside down! Inversions involve putting your heart above your head or going upside down. They are a part of every yoga class. Children find inversions exciting and thrilling, but their teachers are often a little hesitant to include them in their yoga class lesson plans. That is interesting because an adult yoga class is full of inversions—and many times adults don't realize they are doing them. Down Dog, Standing Forward Fold, or Ragdoll are all common poses in a yoga class, and they are all inversions.

Of course some inversions are more difficult than others such as headstands, handstands, and Firefly Pose, but remember yoga is a lifelong practice and there is always something to work toward.

Often in an adult yoga class when the instructor guides everyone into a headstand or Crow Pose, a little fear and trepidation sneaks in for adults. We are afraid of losing our balance, falling, and making a fool of ourselves. Guess what? Kids are the opposite of us in that regard and have little or no fear of trying inversions. Most kids love trying to go upside down and don't hesitate to try it again if they fall.

Benefits of Inversions

Learning and knowing the numerous benefits of doing inversions will help teachers add a few to their classes. Start slowly. There are lots of different types of inversions and all will give benefit. There is no need to hold a perfect headstand for three minutes to gain the benefits of inversions.

I tell my students that doing inversions will refresh their blood and make them smarter. When your body is upside down, and your feet are higher than your heart, the normal pull of gravity on your body is reversed, which helps return blood to the heart.

Inversions can also make you happy! Endorphins are released and your frown will literally be turned upside down. Kids are usually pretty good about not taking themselves too seriously. They will fall but then laugh and get right back up again to try.

Remember that safety is important when teaching inversions. There will always be some students in a yoga kids class who will try to whip right into a headstand as soon as you say the word, but you must be ready for that and have them watch and listen to directions first. Take the students through the pose step by step and allow them to see the proper technique so they can practice correctly and safely.

Inversions That Kids Can Practice:

Bridge Pose

Wheel Pose

More Inversions to Try:
- Legs up the Wall
- Shoulder Stand
- Crow
- Side Crow
- Handstand Kick Up
- Tripod Headstand

How to Teach Headstands

I really like this simple order to teach kids how to do a headstand. I have also helped many kids achieve a tripod or headstand with the simple tip of placing their hands in front of their heads to gain more leverage and balance.

1. Place mat against wall.
2. Place the very top flat part of your head on your mat. The back of head should be against the wall.
3. Place your hands in front of your head so you are able to see all 10 fingers. This gives more space for balancing.
4. Go into a Tripod Pose first. Lift your legs slowly.
5. Flex your feet so they are flat as if stamping the wall.
6. Pull your core tight and utilize the wall for support if needed.

Use the wall when teaching handstands as well. Many people don't think about using a wall, but knowing it is there if needed and having the extra support can build confidence.

My own kids, who are not gymnastically inclined, love kicking up into a handstand against the wall in our living room. There are lots of wall thumps as they kick into a handstand, but I'm just happy they give it a go. Try it with the kids. You may surprise yourself!

Part 9: Build Community

Building Community comes toward the end of the yoga class. Everyone has had fun, learned a lot, and now it is time to bring it to a close. As a teacher, it can be tempting to skip or rush this portion of class if you are feeling short on time. I encourage you to really make time for this building community portion of class. It is a very important part for your students as well as for you, their teacher.

It is incredibly beneficial to reflect on what you have learned as a class and to give the students a chance to share, connect, and work together one final time. The kids enjoy this part of class as you review all they have done together. It makes them feel more united and stronger together.

This is personally one of my favorite parts of class as it ties everything together. The students talk about what they learned and what they enjoyed. I'm always surprised to hear what the students' favorite parts of class were. Often, it is not what I think such as mastering a difficult pose, but instead it might be how they felt or how they connected with another student and maybe made a new friend.

The following are a few ideas for Building Community. Remember you only need a few minutes to come together as a community to make this effective. It doesn't take long so don't miss it!

Ideas for Building Community

Circle Showcase: This is the child's chance to showcase a favorite pose in front of everyone. Let each child take a turn to pick any pose they learned in class and show it off in the center of the mat circle.

Pass the Squeeze: Students sit up tall in a circle while holding hands. The first person squeezes the person's hand next to them and says a word that describes how they feel—happy, peaceful, special, calm. Continue around the circle. This can also be done with just passing the squeeze without saying any words. Students are usually mesmerized and silent while watching the squeeze work its way through the circle.

This is truly a beautiful way to build community within a group with little effort.

Rain Orchestra: Create a thunderstorm while sitting in a circle with the lights on low. It is a wonderful exercise to utilize almost all of the senses. The leader begins with Step 1, and the students follow. For older kids, you can make the building and receding of the storm more gradual since they do not switch steps until the person sitting next to them does.

How to Create a Thunderstorm:

1. Rub your hands together
2. Snap your fingers
3. Clap your hands
4. Slap your hands on your legs. At this time a student could flick a light switch on and off to represent lightning
5. Stomp your feet
6. Slap your hands on your legs and stomp your feet. This represents the height of the storm
7. Stomp your feet
8. Slap your hands on your legs
9. Clap your hands
10. Snap fingers
11. Rub your hands together
12. Open palms (quiet)

Sharing Circle: In your community circle, let each student take a turn sharing a word or phrase that describes how he or she is feeling at that moment. Often times I am surprised at the insightfulness of the students as they relay words expressing calm, peacefulness, contentedness, strength, or relaxation. This exercise helps promote a good feeling of self-awareness, peace, and empathy toward others. They are simple words, but they are powerful and help students carry that feeling and awareness outside of class.

The teacher and parent part of me also enjoys the Building Community portion of class. It is the perfect refresher and helps the kids remember what they did during class so they can share with their parents. Another way to do this is through your parent communication notes (See examples in Chapter 5). As a parent I love hearing exactly what my children learned and did in their classes. It gives me the opportunity to encourage them to practice at home and show others. All of this helps build better retention skills and lasting memories.

Part 10: Stillness and Savasana

Ahh… you made it to the final part of your kids yoga class! Now it is time for the students to rest, relax, and reap all of the benefits from their hard work. Savasana often becomes the children's favorite part of class, which I think is incredible since it is the part where they are not doing a thing. The students begin class so eager, excited, and full of energy, and then after moving and working their bodies in such a good and healthy way, they really are ready for rest and relaxation. I tell my students their bodies deserve this rest and that taking this time helps them repair and build the muscles they just worked.

Please do not get the idea that when I call out, "Time for Savasana" the kids readily roll onto their backs, shut their eyes, and go into deep stillness. Savasana must be gradually built into the class flow. It follows the Building Community portion of class so the students are already settling down and reflecting on what they have done and accomplished during class.

How to Effectively Get Children Into Savasana

1. Turn the lights down low.
2. Begin to play slower and more calming music or nature sounds.
3. Have students sit tall with their legs straight out in front of them.
4. Challenge them to lie down as slowly as they can while counting down from 10. I tell older students to allow each vertebrate to touch the mat one at a time.
5. Once they are lying down, have the children stretch out as long as they can on their mats with their arms stretched out above them and their toes pointed.
6. Next, have them curl up into a ball and give their knees a hug. Their legs have worked hard and deserve the love.
7. Allow the students to lay however they feel comfortable—on their backs, stomachs, or curled into a ball. Sometimes the students place their yoga mats over top of them as if they are in a little cave.

8. Using phrases such as "Be as still as a statue" or "Quiet as a mouse" gives the students a mental picture of how to pose and act.
9. During Savasana, I sometimes like to lightly rub the students' backs. It is amazing the calm it brings and how much they respond to this little touch.

Bringing Kids Out of Savasana:

Your first few yoga classes will have students peeking around, fidgeting, or even fake snoring during Savasana. Stick with it though! As you continue to make your expectations clear and follow a similar format each class, your students will definitely begin to settle down faster and easier as they anticipate this final resting pose.

After a few moments, which can range from 30 seconds to two minutes depending on the age and maturity of your class, it is time to bring them out of Savasana. I decrease the volume of music slowly, have them roll over to their sides, and use their arms as pillows.

Slowly have your students sit up, cross-legged, with their eyes shut. Lead the class through a few cleansing breaths with arms outstretched overhead and then bring their hands back to heart center. I like to give a few positive closing words that unite the class and set their path for the remainder of the day or the week. I also like to thank them for coming to yoga, taking care of their bodies, working together, and having fun. If this is a series of classes definitely tell them that you cannot wait to see them on their mats next time. Namaste.

Chapter 4: Yoga Kids Themed Lesson Plans

The following fifteen lesson plans are ready to go and use with your yoga students! You can rest assured that they are kid-tried and -tested lessons, which have been implemented many times. Kids enjoy yoga classes that are based on fun themes and are energetic and engaging. I have found that having a theme for your yoga class makes it easier for students to learn and recall all that they have learned and done in class. Feel free to make any changes to modify or differentiate based on the needs and levels of your students.

Each part of the lesson plans follow themes and ideas discussed in the previous chapter. It is easy to swap out a Breath Work idea, Active Movement exercise, or another Yoga Game (Chapter 3) if you have another that you would like to try.

Theme:	Blast Off
Ages:	3-6
Materials:	Items for the yoga obstacle course
Welcome: (3 minutes)	What do you know about space?
Breath Work: (2 minutes)	**Rocket Breath:** Students breathe in and out through their noses deeply while you, the teacher, count down from 10. When you hit one, say "Blast off," and the students exhale through their mouths.
Sun Salutation: (3 minutes)	**Sun A**
Active Movement: (5 minutes)	• **Gravity Jumps:** squat jumps • **Moon Walk:** around the room • **Shooting Star:** Star jumps are similar to jumping jacks but you jump back up as if on a trampoline.
Theme Poses: (5-10 minutes)	• **Sun:** Mountain Pose with arms stretched overhead • **Rocket:** Chair Pose • **Star Pose** • **Half Moon Pose**
Game: (10 minutes)	**Space Race:** Create an obstacle course with whatever objects you have available. Hula Hoops laid on the ground to do high knees through, jump ropes laid parallel that kids need to jump across, cones to jump over or hop to, and yoga blocks for stepping or jumping over. I like to put all of my "obstacles" in a large circle with a yoga mat and theme pose cards after each obstacle. The kids move around the obstacle course and perform the yoga poses that are shown on cards and hold for five breaths or 30 seconds. This is also fun to

	do to music. See if they can get faster each time.
Partner/Group Challenge Poses: (10 minutes) **OR** **Inversion/Balance:** (10 minutes)	**Rocket:** Partners face one another about an arm's length apart. They touch their palms together above and press into each other. Each partner takes a small step backward. They should keep taking small steps until they reach a mutual point and then raise their hands up together to form the top of a rocket.
Community Closing: (2 minutes)	**Super Star:** Have each student showcase their favorite pose in the center of the circle.
Stillness and Savasana: (5 minutes)	Students pretend as if they are floating in space and lie as still as they can.

Theme:	Brown Bear, Brown Bear
Ages:	3-6
Materials:	*Brown Bear, Brown Bear, What Do You See?* by Eric Carle
Welcome: (3 minutes)	What is your favorite animal? Why?
Breath Work: (2 minutes)	Students breathe in and out deeply as if they are bears hibernating through winter.
Sun Salutation: (3 minutes)	**Sun A**
Active Movement: (5 minutes)	Everyone follows the leader with different animal walks around the room—bear walks, horses galloping, frog jumps, etc.
Theme Poses: (5-10 minutes)	Read *Brown Bear, Brown Bear, What Do See?* When you get to each different animal in the book, pause and have the students practice that pose. <ul><li>**Bear** (Bear walk in place)</li><li>**Bird** (Warrior 3)</li><li>**Duck** (Duck Pose)</li><li>**Horse** (Horse Pose)</li><li>**Frog** (Frog Pose)</li><li>**Cat** (Cat Pose)</li><li>**Dog** (Down Dog)</li><li>**Fish** (Fish Pose)</li></ul>
Game: (10 minutes)	**Freeze Dance:** Students dance around the room and when the music goes off, freeze in one of the learned poses.
Partner/Group Challenge Poses: (10 minutes) OR Inversion/Balance: (10 minutes)	Each student holds their favorite pose for 10 seconds. When the time is up, they must change to a different pose.
Community Closing:	**Name that Pose:** Each child takes a

(2 minutes)	turn showing a pose that they learned. See how quickly the other students can guess it.
Stillness and Savasana: (5 minutes)	Everyone picks a favorite animal from the book, giving them time to rest. For example, the bear goes into his cave, dog in the dog house, cat relaxing in the sun, or a bird in a nest.

Theme:	Mythical Creatures
Ages:	3-12
Materials:	Handkerchief (or some other easy to hold object to be the "jewels") Glitter (optional)
Welcome: (3 minutes)	Brainstorm imaginary creatures that are fun to pretend with such as a unicorn, dragon, or fairy.
Breath Work: (2 minutes)	**Dragon's Breath:** Students breathe in through their noses as a dragon would and then let a giant breath out through their mouths as if breathing fire.
Sun Salutation: (3 minutes)	**Sun A**
Active Movement: (5 minutes)	**Catch the Dragon by the Tail:** Have the students stand in a line while holding hands. The leader tries to catch the other end of the line while still holding hands. Switch leaders often. If they are having difficulty catching the tail, you can help them by moving into a smaller circle formation, which makes this easier.
Theme Poses: (5-10 minutes)	<ul><li>**Dragon:** Triangle Pose</li><li>**Unicorn:** Goddess Pose (with hands on head to make a unicorn horn)</li><li>**Fairy:** Dancer's Pose</li><li>**Castle:** Down Dog</li></ul>
Game: (10 minutes)	**Smaug's Jewels:** The dragon stands in the middle of the circle and guards the "jewels," which can be any object such as a handkerchief or a bean bag. The rest of the students try to steal the "jewels" by reaching in. If they are tagged by Smaug they

	must freeze in a yoga pose until someone untags them. This works well in groups of 4-8.
Partner/Group Challenge Poses: (10 minutes) **OR** **Inversion/Balance:** (10 minutes)	**King and Peasants:** The students become the "peasants" and sit in a circle while the "king" turns his back and waits in a corner. Next choose one student to be the leader. The leader moves in and out of yoga poses while the rest of the peasants follow. The king returns to the center of the circle and tries to guess who the leader is. Give the king three guesses before choosing a new king and leader.
Community Closing: (2 minutes)	**Circle Showcase:** This is each child's chance to showcase a favorite pose in front of everyone. Let everyone take a turn to pick any pose that they learned and show it off in the center of the circle.
Stillness and Savasana: (5 minutes)	Sprinkle imaginary fairy dust (glitter) on the students as they lie on their yoga mats and go into a deep "sleep."

Theme:	Yoga Bugs
Ages:	3-6
Materials:	Music
Welcome: (3 minutes)	How many bugs can you think of?
Breath Work: (2 minutes)	**Bug Breath**: Students inhale (hold for a count of three) and then exhale.
Sun Salutation: (3 minutes)	**Sun A**
Active Movement: (5 minutes)	<ul><li>Bug walk across the room</li><li>Slide like a snail</li><li>Jump like a cricket</li><li>Fly like a ladybug</li><li>March like an ant</li><li>Roll like a roly poly</li></ul>
Theme Poses: (5-10 minutes)	<ul><li>**Butterfly Pose**</li><li>**Dead Bug Pose**</li><li>**Locust Pose**</li></ul>
Game: (10 minutes)	**Bed Bugs:** The children dance, move, and hop to music as if they are bed bugs. When the music stops, all bugs need to freeze.
Partner/Group Challenge Poses: (10 minutes) OR Inversion/Balance: (10 minutes)	**Spider's Web:** Similar to a human knot, have the kids stand in a circle and grab hands across the circle and try to get out of the knot without letting go of hands. To make this less challenging for younger kids have a few students at the start hold the person's hand next to them instead of everyone going across the circle to grab a hand.
Community Closing: (2 minutes)	**Bug Collector:** Let each student take a turn demonstrating a pose of a bug that they would like to collect.
Stillness and Savasana: (5 minutes)	**Reclining Butterfly:** Everyone lies on their backs and brings the soles of their feet together.

Theme:	Ocean Fun
Ages:	3-6
Materials:	Music
Welcome: (3 minutes)	Who has been to the ocean? What did you see?
Breath Work: (2 minutes)	**Breathe Like Waves:** Students let their breath move in and out as if they are an ocean wave. They should count how long it takes and see if they can make their exhales longer each time.
Sun Salutation: (3 minutes)	**Deep Sea Diver:** Everyone breathes in with arms outstretched above their heads. Next, they breathe out and pretend to be diving off a cliff and into the ocean. Repeat several times.
Active Movement: (5 minutes)	Crab walks up and down yoga mats or around the room.
Theme Poses: (5-10 minutes)	<ul><li>**Boat Pose**</li><li>**Dolphin Pose**</li><li>**Heron Pose**</li><li>**Fish Pose**</li><li>**Mermaid:** (Updog Pose)</li></ul>
Game: (10 minutes)	**Musical Mats:** Place yoga mats in a circle and play music as students move around the mats in a circle. When the music stops they must choose a mat and hold an ocean themed pose.
Partner/Group Challenge Poses: (10 minutes) OR Inversion/Balance: (10 minutes)	**Submarine:** Partners stand facing one another and hold one another's wrists, leaning back so they are each supporting one another. Partners then bend knees until they are parallel to the floor. Have them try to go back up and down as if they are submarines in the ocean. **Variation:** Students sit back to back with arms hooked. First, have them practice back to back breathing and then

	try to stand up without unhooking arms.
Community Closing: (2 minutes)	**Group Boat:** Everyone sits close together in a circle holding hands with the person next to them and moving into Boat Pose. Talk about how they are stronger together.
Stillness and Savasana: (5 minutes)	Students spread out like starfish on their yoga mats and relax.
Bonus Game:	**Ship/Shore:** Make a line down the middle. The leader calls out ship or shore and the students jump to that side. Keep the game moving quickly to try and trick the children. Once in a while interject an ocean yoga pose, and everyone must break into that pose.

Theme:	Off to the Zoo!
Ages:	3-6
Materials:	None
Welcome: (3 minutes)	Which animals live in the zoo?
Breath Work: (2 minutes)	**Elephant:** Everyone stands with their feet apart. Clasp hands in front to make an elephant trunk and bend at the waist. Inhale through the nose as they raise arms up over their heads and lean back. Next, they exhale through their mouths as they swing their arms down through their legs. Repeat several times.
Sun Salutation: (3 minutes)	**Sun A**
Active Movement: (5 minutes)	**Animal Walks:** Students start at one end of the room and practice different animal walks across the room such as monkey, crab, bear, and frog.
Theme Poses: (5-10 minutes)	• **Giraffe:** Tree Pose with arms extended overhead • **Alligator:** lay on belly and "chomp" with arms • **Elephant:** one-armed Down Dog • **Cobra:** Cobra Pose • **Lion:** Cat Pose on all fours and let out a roar!
Game: (10 minutes)	**Yogi Says:** Similar to Simon Says, the leader calls out different actions or yoga poses—pat head, jump in place, touch toes, Elephant Pose, Giraffe Pose, etc. The leader chooses to preface the movement with "Yogi says" or not.
Partner/Group Challenge	**Group Cobra:** Everyone lies on

Poses: (10 minutes) **OR** **Inversion/Balance:** (10 minutes)	their stomachs in a close circle. As they raise their heads and hands into Cobra Pose, they should touch their palms to the person on either side on them.
Community Closing: (2 minutes)	**Zoo Animal Exhibit:** At the same time, everyone goes into their favorite zoo animal and makes the correlating animal sound. This creates an engaging and noisy exhibit.
Stillness and Savasana: (5 minutes)	Students stretch out long and still like a snake and are very, very sssssstill.

Theme:	Frozen Yoga Fun
Ages:	3-12
Materials:	Music, magic wand (optional)
Welcome: (3 minutes)	What are your favorite things to do in the snow?
Breath Work: (2 minutes)	Students breathe in and out through their noses and mouths as if fogging up the mirror.
Sun Salutation: (3 minutes)	Sun A
Active Movement: (5 minutes)	Everyone lies on their backs and passes ice blocks (yoga blocks) between their hands and feet in a sit-up position.
Theme Poses: (5-10 minutes)	• **Snowflake:** Star Pose • **Hero to save the day**: Warrior II Pose • **Troll:** Child's Pose • **Snow Queen:** Dancer Pose
Game: (10 minutes)	**Frozen Dance:** Play music while everyone dances around. Stop the music and the Snow Queen announces a pose and then freezes subjects into that pose with her hand or wand. Everyone holds the pose until the music starts again. Take turns with passing the wand to the next person.
Partner/Group Challenge Poses: (10 minutes) OR Inversion/Balance: (10 minutes)	**Rooftops:** Make ice castles with a partner. Have each partner stand facing each other a foot apart and press hands together to form a rooftop. Slowly take steps back.
Community Closing: (2 minutes)	**Snow Monster Chase:** The group stands in a circle and passes the Hula Hoop while holding hands. hands and see how fast the group can pass

	it.
Stillness and Savasana: (5 minutes)	Everyone pretends they are a piece of ice and are melting into the ground.

Theme:	Let it Snow!
Ages:	3-12
Materials:	Small yarn balls or Styrofoam balls 3 to 4 inches in diameter. Use masking tape or duct tape to write yoga poses onto the tape with a permanent marker. Attach the tape to the balls.
Welcome: (3 minutes)	What are your favorite activities to do in the snow?
Breath Work: (2 minutes)	It's cold outside. Warm up from the inside. Students breathe in deeply through their noses. Instruct them to keep their lips together and exhale as long as they can. Do that several times and see if they start a little fire or warmth in their bellies.
Sun Salutation: (3 minutes)	**Sun A**
Active Movement: (5 minutes)	**Snowball Fight!** Everyone loves a good old-fashioned snowball fight. Put a line down the middle of the room and form two teams on either side of line. Announce "Ready set go!" and everyone can begin throwing snowballs across the line. When the leader says, "Freeze," children must pick a snowball and hold that pose as quickly as they can. Hold the pose until the snowball fight begins again.
Theme Poses: (5-10 minutes)	Any of the poses that are written on the snowballs will work well to learn and practice. This is a wonderful way to learn a variety of poses. I like to let students pick two to three snowballs and show those poses to everyone. Older students can transition smoothly between the poses.
Game:	**Snowball Toss:** Have them pick a

(10 minutes)	partner and stand a foot apart and toss the snowball to one another without dropping it. Each partner takes a step back after each toss. Pause and perform a yoga pose after each toss. See how far apart they can get without dropping the snowball.
Partner/Group Challenge Poses: (10 minutes) **OR** **Inversion/Balance:** (10 minutes)	**Balance Your Snowball:** Each student chooses a snowball and practices balancing it on their heads, shoulders, and elbows as they walk across the room. See if they can balance it on their heads while trying balance poses such as Tree, Airplane, and Dancer.
Community Closing: (2 minutes)	**Snowball Gather:** One person holds a strong Boat Pose, which becomes their snowball buckets. Put as many snowballs in each person's "bucket" as they can hold without letting them drop. Take turns filling one another's bucket with snowballs.
Stillness and Savasana: (5 minutes)	Have them pretend to be snowballs on a hot day and melt slowly into their mats.

Theme:	Egg-cellent Spring Kids Yoga
Ages:	3-12
Materials:	Colored plastic eggs, basket Have the following poses typed or written, cut, and put one in each egg. <ul><li>**Robin:** Airplane Pose</li><li>**Duck:** Duck Pose. Encourage students to flap, quack, and waddle around like a duck.</li><li>**Sun:** Mountain Pose with arms outstretched to the sun</li><li>**Spring Hat:** Down Dog</li><li>**Spring Tree:** Tree Pose</li><li>**Rainbow:** Bridge Pose</li><li>**Spring Basket:** Boat Pose</li><li>**Flower:** Lotus Pose. Make petals by having the children hold their arms above their heads.</li><li>**Caterpillar:** Locust Pose. Have the students raise and lower their heads as if eating leaves.</li><li>**Butterfly:** Butterfly Pose. Fly butterflies fast and then slow.</li><li>**Bunny:** Hero Pose. Have the children make bunny ears with their hands.</li></ul>
Welcome: (3 minutes)	What is your favorite thing about spring? Why?
Breath Work: (2 minutes)	**Bunny Breath:** Students sit up tall in Hero Pose with hands resting open on their knees. They take three sniffs in with their noses (like a bunny) and then one large exhale through their mouths.

Sun Salutation: (3 minutes)	Sun A
Active Movement: (5 minutes)	**Spring Egg Pass:** The students sit in a circle and play music. The students pass one plastic egg as quickly as possible around the circle. When the music stops, the child holding the egg makes the yoga pose that is written inside the egg. As the children master this game using a single egg try using two or three eggs at a time.
Theme Poses: (5-10 minutes)	The students take turns picking an egg and learning and demonstrating the pose (listed above in Materials) that they find inside.
Game: (10 minutes)	**Spring Egg Balance:** Each student selects an egg. Everyone lines up on one side of the room and tries walking across the room with these different balance poses. • On outstretched hand • On top of head • In between shoulder and ear • In the crook of elbow • In between knees
Partner/Group Challenge Poses: (10 minutes) OR Inversion/Balance: (10 minutes)	**Spring Egg Gather:** In partners, have one student make a spring basket (Boat Pose). The other student places eggs in their "basket." Try to gather as many as possible without the plastic eggs falling out.
Community Closing: (2 minutes)	**Spring Egg Pass:** Sit in a close circle. One student puts an egg in between their feet. They must then pass the egg around the circle with their feet. This is great teamwork and core strengthening.

Stillness and Savasana: (5 minutes)	Have the students see how still they can lie with an egg on their stomachs. Tell them to relax and watch their stomachs rise and fall as they breathe deeply.

Theme:	Super Hero Yoga
Ages:	3-6
Materials:	Items for "Save the City" obstacle course
Welcome: (3 minutes)	Which superheroes do you know? Who would you like to be? Why?
Breath Work: (2 minutes)	Students breathe in and out deeply like the Incredible Hulk.
Sun Salutation: (3 minutes)	**Sun A**
Active Movement: (5 minutes)	Superheroes must build their strength! Have them do 10 reps of varying exercises such as jumping jacks, push-ups, and sit-ups.
Theme Poses: (5-10 minutes)	<ul><li>**Catwoman:** Cat Pose into Cow Pose. Students should arch their backs and remember to breathe.</li><li>**Superman:** Have them lie on their stomachs and stretch their arms out in front of them. Can they move them as if they are flying?</li><li>**Spiderman:** Plank Pose. Can the students lift their hands and legs as if walking up a wall?</li><li>**Elasti-Girl:** Warrior 2. Students should stretch their arms as far as they can!</li></ul>
Game: (10 minutes)	**Superhero Obstacle Course:** Save the City! Use what you have on hand and set items up in a circle. The point is to create challenges for your super heroes to complete. 1. Cross tall buildings (yoga blocks) 2. Jump over burning flames

	(jump ropes laid parallel on ground) 3. Roll under speeding cars (yoga mats in line) 4. Balance through laser lights (stepping on beanbags)
Partner/Group Challenge Poses: (10 minutes) **OR** **Inversion/Balance:** (10 minutes)	Students lie in a circle on their stomachs in Superman Pose, joining hands with those next to them. Can they lift their arms and legs together as if flying?
Community Closing: (2 minutes)	Review the poses they have learned. Which other super powers and poses do they think superheroes would use?
Stillness and Savasana: (5 minutes)	All of the superheroes have worked so hard to save the world! Time to give their bodies a rest on their mats.

Theme:	Valentine Yoga
Ages:	3-6
Materials:	Yarn
Welcome: (3 minutes)	How do you show others that you love them?
Breath Work: (2 minutes)	**Back to Back Partner Breathing:** Students sit back to back with a partner and synchronize their deep breaths so they are able to feel their partner's inhales and exhales.
Sun Salutation: (3 minutes)	**Sun A:** Students open their hearts on the inhale as they stretch high with their hands above their heads and lean back so their hearts are open.
Active Movement: (5 minutes)	**Make your heart strong!** Everyone chooses an exercise to get their hearts pumping. Choose between squat jumps, jumping jacks, and mountain climbers.
Theme Poses: (5-10 minutes)	• **Cupid** (Warrior 2): Instruct students to pull one arm back and forth as if releasing an arrow. • **Arrow Pose** (Side Plank Pose): Have students bend the top leg as it is resting on their calves. • **Bow Pose** • **Flower Pose**
Game: (10 minutes)	**Friendship Web:** Sit in a circle with a ball of yarn. Give a compliment to one student such as "I like how you always try your best," and pass the yarn to them while holding onto the end. The child that is holding the yarn then compliments another student and

	passes the yarn. This creates a beautiful friendship web that your students will definitely remember.
Partner/Group Challenge Poses: (10 minutes) **OR** **Inversion/Balance:** (10 minutes)	**Open Heart:** Students stand behind a partner with one foot back and one foot forward, bending knees slightly. They should hold their partner's wrists, while the partner leans forward and opens and shines their heart forward.
Community Closing: (2 minutes)	**Pass the Squeeze:** Students sit up tall in a circle while holding hands. The first person squeezes the person's hand next to them, continuing around the circle. Students are usually mesmerized and silent while watching the squeeze work its way through the circle. This is truly a beautiful way to build community within a group with little effort.
Stillness and Savasana: (5 minutes)	Instruct students to lie on their yoga mats and draw their knees in to give themselves a big hug. Their bodies have worked hard and they deserve some love! Tell them to slowly let go and let their bodies and hearts melt into Savasana.

Theme:	Welcome to the Jungle
Ages:	3-12
Materials:	Music
Welcome: (3 minutes)	What is your favorite animal that lives in the jungle? Why?
Breath Work: (2 minutes)	**Elephant Breath:** Students stand with their feet hip distance apart and clasp their hands in front to make an elephant trunk, bending at the waist. Instruct them to inhale through their noses as they raise their arms up over their heads and lean back. They then exhale through their mouths as they swing their arms down through their legs. Repeat several times.
Sun Salutation: (3 minutes)	**Sun A**
Active Movement: (5 minutes)	**Animal Walks:** gorilla, monkey walk, snake **Trip through the jungle:** Students pretend to jump over logs, duck under branches, high knees through quicksand, run from the tiger, tiptoe past a snake, and swing through trees like Tarzan.
Theme Poses: (5-10 minutes)	• **Lion** (Cat Pose to Cow Pose): "Roar" on the exhale • **Cobra:** Cobra Pose • **Giraffe:** Tree Pose with arms extended above • **Elephant:** One-armed Down Dog. Swing your "trunk" from side to side.
Game:	**Hunter:** Move around the room

(10 minutes)	to music. When the music stops, everyone chooses a pose that was just learned and holds it as still as possible. The "hunter" walks around to see which animal is moving. The "hunter" will then choose an animal by tapping them and that child becomes the new "hunter." Everyone then moves around to music and freezes into a new pose when the music stops.
Partner/Group Challenge Poses: (10 minutes) **OR** **Inversion/Balance:** (10 minutes)	**Partner Cobra:** Students go into Cobra Pose while facing one another with hands pressed against one another and lift up. **Group Tree:** Stand in Tree Pose in a circle with hands held together or on one another's shoulders.
Community Closing: (2 minutes)	**Create a Thunderstorm** Sit in a circle and give the directions below: <ul><li>Rub your hands together.</li><li>Snap your fingers.</li><li>Clap your hands.</li><li>Slap your hands on your legs. For extra fun, a student can flick a light switch on and off to represent lightning.</li><li>Stomp your feet.</li></ul> Reverse this order by going back up and finish with open palms for quiet.
Stillness and Savasana: (5 minutes)	Everyone lies as still and quiet as a little jungle mouse.

Theme:	Winter Olympics
Ages:	3-12
Materials:	Paper plates, Hula Hoop, feathers, yoga pose cards
Welcome: (3 minutes)	What are your favorite Winter Olympic sports?
Breath Work: (2 minutes)	**Feather Fun Race:** Olympic athletes need to have a strong breath to help them compete at top level. Have a mini competition with feathers to practice Breath Work. Give each student a feather and have them line up on one end of the room. While moving across the room on their hands and knees, they need to blow their feather to the finish line.
Sun Salutation: (3 minutes)	**Sun A**
Active Movement: (5 minutes)	**Speed Skating** (use paper plates): Give each student two paper plates that they place under their feet. Have them glide and slide around the room.
Theme Poses: (5-10 minutes)	• **Skier** (Chair Pose): Everyone holds their arms out in front of them, as they move their arms as if they are holding ski poles. This pose can also be a speed skater as they move their arms back and forth. • **Bobsled** (Boat Pose): Sway right and left as if on a sled. • **Ice Skater** (Airplane Pose): Children put a leg straight behind them as if they are gliding down the ice.

	• **Snowboarder** (Warrior 2): Students jump midair in this position as they switch lead legs. Try to have some "hang time."
Game: **(10 minutes)**	**Mini Olympics:** Set up a short obstacle course with cones, hoops, or anything else you have on hand. Place yoga pose cards between some of the obstacles. Have each student take a turn competing in the Mini Olympics. Time them if you like.
Partner/Group Challenge Poses: **(10 minutes)** **OR** **Inversion/Balance:** **(10 minutes)**	**Hula Hoop Pass:** Have the students stand in a circle and hold hands. Pass the Hula Hoop around the circle without letting go of hands.
Community Closing: **(2 minutes)**	Have each student showcase a favorite pose and announce if they won a gold medal by doing the best that they can.
Stillness and Savasana: **(5 minutes)**	Everyone relaxes their Olympic bodies on the mat. They deserve it!

Theme:	Yoga Pet Store
Ages:	3-6
Materials:	Slips of paper with different pets written on them. Examples are cat, dog, bird, horse, and snake.
Welcome: (3 minutes)	What kind of pets do you have? Would you like to have?
Breath Work: (2 minutes)	**Snake Breath:** Students sit up tall and take a deep breath in through their noses to fill up their whole bodies. They then breathe out slowly and make a hissing sound like a snake for as long as they can with their tongues up against the roofs of their mouths. Repeat several times.
Sun Salutation: (3 minutes)	**Sun A**
Active Movement: (5 minutes)	**Pets on the Loose:** Have the children move around the room to music. When the music stops, they must freeze in an animal pose.
Theme Poses: (5-10 minutes)	<ul><li>**Dog:** Down Dog Pose</li><li>**Cat:** Cat Pose</li><li>**Snake:** Cobra Pose</li><li>**Rabbit:** Rabbit Pose</li><li>**Mouse:** Child's Pose</li><li>**Fish:** Fish Pose</li><li>**Frog:** Malasana Pose</li><li>**Lizard:** Plank Pose</li><li>**Bird:** Warrior 3</li><li>**Horse:** Goddess Pose</li></ul>
Game: (10 minutes)	**Yoga Pet Store:** Put the yoga mats in a long line. Everyone draws a card with an animal pose listed above. They strike the pose on their yoga mats. The "customer" walks up and down the aisle to choose which

	pose or animal they want to buy. That child becomes the next customer in the pet store. Everyone draws a new card.
Partner/Group Challenge Poses: **(10 minutes)** **OR** **Inversion/Balance:** **(10 minutes)**	**Double Down Dog:** One partner goes into Down Dog. The other partner stands in front of them and goes into Down Dog. The front partner places one foot on their partner's lower back and slowly brings their other foot up to meet it. Younger students will need assistance with getting their feet up to their partner's back. If the partners are comfortable in this pose then have them switch spots. This partner pose can also be done as a large group and looks pretty fantastic when mastered.
Community Closing: **(2 minutes)**	**Circle Showcase:** Everyone picks their favorite animal pose and showcases it in the center of the circle.
Stillness and Savasana: **(5 minutes)**	Be as quiet as a mouse.

Chapter 5: Parent Communication

Have you ever asked a child what they did at school, camp, or class and heard "I don't remember" or "Nothing"? I find that disheartening both as a teacher and a parent since I know that is rarely the case. Children are actively engaged and experience a lot in any given situation.

I love hearing my children's thoughts on their experiences. I have found that asking, "What did you do in school today?" is too open ended and broad. Instead, try asking a more specific question such as "Which game did you play in Physical Education?" or "What was the book about that your teacher read?" This type of question will draw out more comments and lead to other items that come to mind.

As a school teacher, I was already aware of the value of parent/teacher communication, and I wanted to carry this on as a yoga instructor. It is important to involve the parents and families so they know what is happening in your yoga class.

The parent notes are not necessary to teach yoga for kids, but it is helpful to think of some way to communicate with your students' families so they know what was covered in class. I have also found that the directors at the places where I teach appreciate my parent notes. They also understand the importance of good communication between class and home.

An Easy Way to Recap

With so much being covered in a 45-60 minute kids yoga class, it is difficult for younger children to remember all of the poses and games that we covered. I find that parent notes can be short but still cover the theme, related poses, games, and any other information I want to pass along. Parents also like this communication because it helps them to later ask their children follow up questions on what they learned.

Sometimes it just takes a word or two to reignite a story or memory from class that day. Kids are usually excited to practice at home what they learned in class and the parent notes give a wonderful framework.

I have included sample parent notes so you can see how simple they can be. It can also differentiate you from other yoga teachers and create a wonderful bridge of communication between your yoga class and families.

Go Go Yoga Kids Parent Note

Theme: Dinosaurs

We had a stompin' and roarin' good time bringing dinosaurs and yoga together. Check out the dinosaur poses that we learned and help practice them at home.

- **Tyrannosaurus Rex** (Chair Pose): Hold your arms out in front and try walking on tiptoes.
- **Brachiosaurs** (Mountain Pose): Stretch your arms as high as you can. Try to reach those leaves!
- **Pterodactyl** (Warrior 3 with arms straight out): Hold your balance as you fly!
- **Stegosaurus** (Dolphin Pose): Imagine you have spikes on your back and take five breaths.

Chair Pose

Mountain Pose

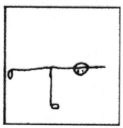

Warrior 3 Pose

Dolphin Pose

Go Go Yoga Kids Parent Note

Theme: Lego Yoga

Which poses can a Lego mini figure perform? Surprisingly a lot! At the beginning of class the children each chose a Lego figure to do yoga with. Many of the poses that can be done with a mini figure went back to the classic standard yoga poses, which are important to revisit. We talked about how these postures are hundreds of years old and were created for reasons such as strength, concentration, and flexibility in our bodies!

Everyone was amazed at how many yoga poses they could create with the Lego figures and their own bodies. We played fun movement games with the "Piece of Resistance" and perfected our Lego jumping jacks. Our balance pose consisted of headstands and our group work involved spelling the word Lego with our bodies.

- **Headstand:** We entered this pose very slowly and practiced safely up against a wall.
- **Down Dog:** This is a classic yoga pose that builds strength and creates flexibility everywhere.
- **Plank Pose:** Can you lift a leg while staying in this pose?
- **Happy Baby Pose:** The kids love this perfectly named pose.

Headstand

Down Dog Pose

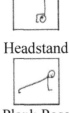
Plank Pose

Happy Baby Pose

Go Go Yoga Kids Parent Note

Theme: Mythical Creatures

Today we used our imaginations and moved our bodies like our favorite mythical creatures. We were dragons, unicorns, and fairies as well as other medieval favorites such as knights, princesses, kings, and queens. We also challenged our balance with Dancer Pose. Ask your child which poses they preferred.

- **Unicorn** (Horse Pose): Put your palms together on top of your head to form a horn.
- **Dragon** (Triangle Pose): Exhale deeply as if breathing fire.
- **Fairy** (Dancer Pose): Find a spot on the ground to focus on as you balance.

  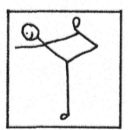

Horse Pose   Triangle Pose   Dancer Pose

Go Go Yoga Kids Parent Note

Theme: Ocean Fun

We had so much fun visiting the ocean today. We warmed up with ocean breathing by letting our breath roll in and out like waves. Next we were ready to crab walk and learn our fun new ocean yoga poses. We also worked on Fish Pose and Crow Pose before becoming submarines and diving deep into the ocean.

- **Boat Pose:** We rowed our boats fast and slow from side to side. We also made our boats go high and low according to the waves. It was amazing core work. Try it!
- **Dolphin Pose:** Dolphin looks like Down Dog, but the balance is on your forearms. This is a very challenging pose to hold!
- **Heron Pose:** Grab your feet and fly through the air. This is another very challenging core and balance pose.

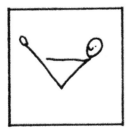      

Boat Pose   Dolphin Pose   Heron Pose

Go Go Yoga Kids Parent Note

Theme: Superheroes

Today we discovered the super powers in all of us as we strengthened our bodies through yoga poses, games, and activities. A favorite was our Save the City obstacle course challenge where we got to practice our poses. Ask your child to show you some of these poses and to tell you about the obstacles that we overcame!

- **Catwoman** (Cat Pose into Cow Pose): Arch your back and then relax.
- **Superman** (Locust Pose): Lie on your stomach and stretch your arms out in front of you. Can you move them as if you are flying?
- **Spiderman** (Plank Pose): Can you move your hands and legs as if walking up a wall?
- **Elasti-Girl** (Warrior 2): Stretch your arms as far as you can!

Locust Pose

Plank Pose

Warrior 2 Pose

Go Go Yoga Kids Parent Note

Theme: Happy Valentine's Day

It is a day filled with love! We shared love, kindness, and friendship with one another by practicing yoga and doing several partner and group activities. Ask your child to tell you about how we opened our hearts, played musical mats, and created a friendship web.

- **Cupid** (Warrior 2): Move your back arm as if drawing an arrow and bring it to meet the front arm.
- **Bow Pose:** Every cupid needs a bow. Can you rock back and forth?
- **Flower Pose** (Lotus Pose): Bring your hands to heart center and make a heart.

 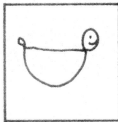 

Warrior 2 Pose   Bow Pose   Lotus Pose

Go Go Yoga Kids Parent Note

Theme: Winter Fun

Today we warmed up our bodies by practicing some winter-related yoga poses, playing freeze dance, and laughing while we tried to ice skate with paper plates. Here are a few poses we worked on. Ask your child to show you some!

- **Snowflake** (Mountain Pose to Standing Forward Fold): Reach for the sky on the inhale and then slowly fall to the ground on the exhale.
- **Ice Skater** (Warrior 3): Find a spot on the ground that is not moving. This will help you hold the pose longer.
- **Snowboard Star** (Warrior 2): Jump 180 degrees and land on your yoga mat.
- **Sled** (Bridge Pose): Can you move your hips side to side as if going down a hill?

Standing Forward Fold

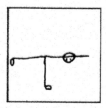

Warrior 3 Pose

Warrior 2 Pose

Bridge Pose

Go Go Yoga Kids Parent Note

Theme: Winter Olympics

Today we were Olympic athletes and competed in a series of challenging yoga poses. We warmed up our bodies by speed skating across the floor. Ask your child what we used as skates (paper plates)! We worked on our new poses and did some fun partner and group challenges. We ended our class with our Yoga Olympic challenge where we did lots of fun poses while we increased our concentration, flexibility, and strength. Since our bodies were good and warm, we practiced Wheel Pose before our final Savasana (resting pose).

- **Skier** (Chair Pose): Put arms out front, take deep breaths, and dig in your poles as you make big turns on the slopes. Become a speed skater in the same pose by moving your arms back and forth
- **Bobsled** (Boat Pose): Move your sled left to right while using your core.
- **Ice Skater** (Warrior 3): Make your body a long line with one leg and both arms stretched out. Remember to keep your balance by looking at something stationary.

Chair Pose

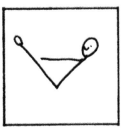

Boat Pose

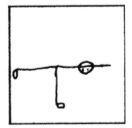

Warrior 3 Pose

Chapter 6: Tweens and Teens Yoga

The tweens and teen age group deserve a category all their own and have a special place in my heart. This age can be awkward but still eager to please. They are not children, nor are they quite adults yet. Their sense of humor and self-discovery are enjoyable. They are really beginning to have their own interests, try things on their own, and test their independence. By adding a repertoire and knowledge of yoga skills, they will be able to use these throughout their lives.

Adolescence is a difficult age. As teens and tweens transform from children to adults, poor body image is a common denominator, which is all the more reason to introduce them to yoga. Yoga builds confidence and strength and helps them feel good inside and out.

Yoga is a Practice

Speak with anyone who loves yoga and notice how they refer to yoga as a "practice." That is because they understand they are constantly learning, trying, and growing through their own personal yoga practice. This is a wonderful notion to introduce to this tween and teen age group—that yoga doesn't expect everyone to be perfect and look like the examples on yoga cards or in magazines. Everyone has a unique body, which will look different in poses, but everyone can receive the benefits and confidence that yoga offers. This is exactly what this age needs, reassurance that different is good!

Health Benefits for Tweens and Teens

Adolescents can be involved in a lot of activities and sports, which can mean a lot of wear and tear on their rapidly growing bodies. I make sure my students know the benefits yoga can have in their daily lives and extracurricular activities. The teens in my classes enjoy hearing about specific professional athletes and teams who regularly practice yoga to be more competitive in their field.

- Yoga builds, lengthens, and tones muscles as poses are held. Kids love hearing how holding Down Dog can actually make them taller as it lengthens the hamstring muscles in the backs of their legs.

- It increases flexibility, which reduces the chance of injury or a pulled muscle during sports.
- Yoga poses work different muscles and each pose has associated health benefits. It is fun to introduce different poses and ask them which parts of their bodies are working. It helps teens to be in tune with their own bodies and how specific poses make them feel.
- Yoga is a stress reliever. Breathing deeply during poses helps you hold poses longer and deeper.
- You can take yoga with you! You always have your breath, which is a great tool to use before a test, game, or competition.
- Yoga makes you feel great inside and out!

Set Up a Tween and Teen Yoga Class

Class structure for a tween and teen class can be set up similar to younger ages with a few modifications.

Tweens typically outgrow the animal or seasonal yoga themes that the younger ages love. They are ready for a more grown-up yoga flow similar to what their parents or other adults do. That said, their classes need to continue to be engaging and specific to their growing and changing bodies. Yoga themes can be centered around friendship, trust, happiness, love, teamwork, balance, core, or inversions. I do encourage you to continue with themes of this nature as it helps to tie and unify your class together.

This age group also enjoys partner, group, and teamwork challenges since they tend to be social and thrive on being together as a group. While working on balance poses and inversions, students achieve satisfaction in working toward a goal and mastering a pose alone or in a group.

This is a wonderful age to get more in-depth with breathing techniques and mindfulness. Teens can become self-absorbed in their world or stressed over school, friends, sports, and other obligations. This is just the nature of this age group. They will outgrow their self-preoccupation over time. Furthermore, with the proper tools and techniques, they will learn in a good yoga class, they will become more mindful and more comfortable with themselves, and they will develop greater empathy toward others.

When I start a new teen class, I first activate their prior knowledge and find out what they know about yoga and any poses they are already familiar with. I also ask them if they are familiar with any of the health benefits of practicing yoga. I know how much their bodies are growing and changing, and by teaching them about the mental and physical benefits of yoga, they'll know how great it is for them.

How to Teach

- **Arrange Mats in a Circle:** This age group really enjoys the community feeling more so than any other age group. The circle set up allows for easier opportunities for sharing ideas and taking turns.
- **Give an Overview:** Adolescents like to know what they are going to be doing in class so it is helpful to give a brief overview at the start of class or post the agenda in some manner. The overview doesn't need to be long and wordy. They just enjoy knowing what is coming next, and it helps them anticipate changes in the class structure.
- **Allow More Time for Sun A and Sun B Salutations**: Teens love to feel as if they are really doing yoga, and helping them build confidence with their yoga flows is one way to do that. Let them know that Sun A and Sun B are what adults are doing in their yoga classes. They also enjoy changing it up a bit by adding on to the flow and taking more time for repetitions while focusing on their breath.
- **Let Them Make Decisions:** Tweens and teens like to feel empowered and have a say in what is going to happen. Feel free to let them be involved in the decision making. This can be achieved with a short discussion on how they are feeling that day and what their bodies may need.

For example, they may have run a mile in PE or have muscles that ache from soccer practice. Having a discussion about how their bodies feel gives them the opportunity to help decide which poses should be sequenced into the yoga flow for that class. While yoga poses are good for almost any body type, some poses are more beneficial for certain areas than others. For example, if they are feeling tightness in their hip flexors or hamstrings this may be a signal to include more hip openers in the yoga flow such as Pigeon Pose or Malasana.

- **Use Yoga Pose Cards:** Teens also enjoy using the yoga pose cards (see Chapter 12) where they select a few yoga posture cards, model them, and then work into the flow. Put the flow to music while going around the circle and taking turns doing everyone's pose. Hold each pose for three to four breaths before moving on to the next one. I like using current pop music during our flow and group work as it makes the class more engaging.
- **Include Yoga Games:** Trust me, this age group still loves to be engaged and learn poses in a game oriented way. Try any of the games listed in the Yoga Games section of Chapter 3. Play a few rounds of the game and move on. Do not use the games for the entire class because the novelty will wear off. Always leave them wanting more!
- **Always Include Partner Poses or Group Challenges:** This age group thrives on being social and working together to accomplish a goal. Partner Poses and Group Challenges allows for just that. Partner Poses look impressive and are fun to do, so introduce them to a new one each class. Favorites from my yoga classes include Human Knot, Double Boat, Elevator, Double Down Dog, and Raindrop. Please refer to the many Partner Poses and Group Challenges in Chapter 3.
- **Inversions and Balance Poses Are Important:** These are often the "party tricks" or magazine poses that people think of when picturing yoga. It is valuable for kids to practice inversions and balance as it often gives them a goal to work

toward.

Just spend a few moments working on Crow Pose, headstand, or another inversion in each class. I let my students know that I did not master these poses on the first try. It took months of strengthening my core, arm muscles, and focus. They will find the balance poses such as Tree Pose and Dancer Pose a little easier to begin with. If they have mastered those, take it up a notch by having them close one or both eyes or shifting their focus to the ceiling.

It is important to get into the habit of always including balance postures in every class since they are at the age where their balance begins to decrease. Make it social by including a Group Tree or Group Airplane Pose. Please refer to the Balance and Inversion ideas in Chapter 3.

- **Close with a Community Circle and Savasana**: I encourage you to not rush this part of class. It will be what the students remember and will leave them with a sense of calm, unity, and accomplishment.

Chapter 7: How to Professionally Teach Yoga for Kids

Now that you are equipped with the knowledge to introduce and teach yoga for kids, it is time to put it into practice. I hope you see how rewarding and fun it can be. With the *Go Go Yoga Kids: Empower Kids for Life Through Yoga* complete resource, a kids yoga teaching certification is not required to teach. Everything you need to know about leading, teaching, and introducing kids to yoga is right here in this guide.

Additional great news is that people in general are becoming more aware of the benefits of yoga and the value of introducing yoga to the youth. The teaching opportunities are out there and will take a little effort, but the reward for the kids (and you) is lifelong. The following are just a few of the places that may offer yoga for kids. If not, you can contact them directly about leading classes.

- Parks and recreation programs in your local area
- Sports and wellness centers such as a YMCA or other health club
- Library programs
- After school programs
- Homeschool and co-op groups
- Preschools
- Daycares
- Fairs/festivals or other children's events
- Yoga studios
- Churches
- Boy Scouts/Girl Scouts
- 4-H clubs

Set Yourself Apart

When I first wanted to teach yoga for kids, I started looking for locations to offer classes. I began with places where I already had a connection. One was a local health club where I was a member and the other was a nearby preschool I had experience with. I called and set up a time to meet with the director of the youth programs. I was prepared with what I was going to say and brought samples of the lessons I would use.

First I outlined the benefits of yoga for kids. I reviewed the structure of the classes I would teach, including what the kids would be learning and doing during their 45 minute class. I had a plan in mind and was prepared and passionate about what I wanted to offer while teaching kids yoga. This gave me confidence and excitement to branch out to other locations.

Another component that helped differentiate me from other youth programs was having a parent communication plan in place. As a teacher who understands the value of parent/teacher communication, I took examples of my yoga parent notes to share with these directors. Please refer to Chapter 5 for more on the importance of having parent notes and pre-made examples. I found the directors appreciated this since they understood the need for good parent communication.

Start Small

When you are just starting out teaching kids yoga at a new location, it is good to offer a 6-8 week session. This is smart for several reasons. It doesn't commit parents, the director, or yourself to a long-term commitment. This is also great for kids as it gives them an opportunity to try something new, learn new skills, and recognize the benefits of yoga. It gives you, as the instructor, the opportunity to step back and evaluate how things went. What would you change for next time? Did the age groups work well? Evaluating after each class helps you improve, change, and build on what you have learned.

Good kids yoga teachers are a special find, and word will travel fast that you are equipped and passionate about reaching all children through yoga. You are in a position to positively influence kids through yoga and introduce them to many lifelong skills and benefits.

Chapter 8: Yoga in the Schools

Most American children today spend the majority of their waking day in school. Now more than ever, schools are responsible for so much more than just content learning. Character education, anti-bullying, test preparation, health, wellness, and incorporating lifelong learning skills are also now part of a regular school day.

We know that schools should be focused on encompassing and enriching the whole child. The good news is that yoga incorporates all of those characteristics! Why not give students the tools they will use through life by incorporating some yoga into their school day?

Yoga for kids is becoming more mainstream in schools. It doesn't even need to be a complete yoga class for kids to achieve the benefits that yoga provides. Through some breathing exercises, mindfulness tips and practice, and simple stress reducing yoga poses, kids will become more focused and attentive and will develop greater empathy toward one another.

As a teacher in the school system I know how full the school day already is with many benchmarks and curriculum guidelines to meet. The last thing most kids need in a competitive school curriculum is another highly structured class. Yoga is not like that. It brings fun, focus, and mindfulness into the classroom and is something all students can participate in and be successful with.

Teachers are incredibly influential in children's lives. They have the opportunity to give students helpful tools they can use throughout life. This is just as important, if not more so, as covering content.

Why Yoga Should Be Included in Schools

- Provides healthy ways for students to express and balance their emotions
- Brings students into the present moment and creates mindfulness, which makes them ready for learning
- Encourages community and teamwork within the classroom
- Helps to create an atmosphere of confidence, enthusiasm, and non-competitiveness where everyone can succeed
- Provides opportunities for beneficial large motor breaks throughout the day in an otherwise mostly sedentary environment
- Eases anxiety and tension (such as pre-test or performance jitters)
- Enhances focus, concentration, comprehension, and memory
- Provides opportunities for reflection and practicing patience
- Improves listening skills
- Engages sluggish minds, which encourages creativity
- Improves posture, which helps students to sit comfortably for longer periods
- Enhances motor skills and balance
- Improves mind/body awareness and connection
- Improves confidence and self-esteem
- Encourages respect for themselves and others
- Creates a calm classroom

All of the above are wonderful benefits that yoga provides. Any teacher would love to have those be part of their classroom! It is also known that classroom management is one of the most common challenges for many teachers. Kids participating in some yoga exercises may be an effective strategy for positively managing classroom behavior.

Change It Up

I have found that student concentration and motivation can easily be improved by changing things up a bit with your class. Do the unexpected, and give students a chance to stretch, move, and work together to achieve a common goal through movement. This in turn boosts student learning, self-esteem, and confidence. Overall it will create a more positive learning environment. Kids are not critiqued, judged, or graded while doing yoga, and it is not competitive. It is just all around healthy for their minds and bodies.

Research has shown that students learn best by taking a break or moving their bodies every 15 minutes. Recess and physical education times are already being reduced in schools, which takes away the active brain breaks that children need. By doing a few yoga exercises concentration and retention can be improved.

In the school classes I teach, I use a lot of guided meditation and imagery to help spur student writing ideas. I have my students close their eyes, take several deep breaths, and be aware of their own mental images before actually writing. This helps my students create more details and description in their writing since they have already imagined it in their heads. This is not an actual up and moving yoga sequence but instead a stationary exercise that can be done from their desks or on the carpet. Guided meditation and imagery have been effective at getting my students to slow down, focus, and concentrate on the task at hand.

Meet the Needs of All Learners

Students learn in different ways, and yoga allows for all different learners to be successful. The kinesthetic learners will be grateful for a chance to move their bodies after time at the carpet, desk, or table. Auditory learners will respond well with the voice cues and explanations. Using yoga pose cards and observing other children doing the poses will help the visual students achieve success. Social learners will enjoy yoga group challenges and partner poses. The sensory aspects of yoga are an opportunity for students to become more aware of their bodies and those around them. There is something for everyone with yoga!

When using yoga in a school classroom it does not need to be a structured class with objectives and benchmarks. There are easy and subtle ways to incorporate the benefits of yoga without taking much time.

Take Mini Yoga Breaks During the School Day

- Introduce new curriculum through yoga poses (ex. an Ocean Unit could include Fish, Boat, Dolphin, and Shark Poses).
- When reading aloud, practice a yoga pose when you come to certain animals or themes. There are many ideas for this in Chapter 4 Themed Lesson Plans.
- Practice breathing techniques to reduce stress and help focus before a test or activity that you know will require concentration and focus. Please refer to the Breath Work ideas for all different ages in Chapter 3.
- Have a student draw a yoga pose card, which everyone will practice during free moments between subjects or while standing in line.
- Invent a new yoga pose to show. Name which parts of the body are working.
- Work with a partner or small group to practice partner poses. Refer to the many partner poses in Chapter 3.
- Play yoga games. There are dozens listed in Chapter 3.
- Do guided visualizations on a specific topic. For example, imagine you are in the rainforest. What do you see and hear?
- For younger ages, recognize seasons changing by doing yoga poses. Be a strong tree or grow from a seed to a flower. There are many ideas for this in Chapter 4: Themed Lesson Plans.
- Introduce a new pose each week. Make it fun! For example, pick a certain word such as your school's name. When you say that word everyone will stop what they are doing and hold that pose.
- Count in a foreign language by fives and 10s while holding a balance pose.
- Take a One Minute Vacation and allow students to shut their eyes, breathe, and visualize themselves in their favorite place.

Try these simple ideas in your classroom and see how your students respond. They will love the change of pace and will be more focused and engaged as they continue with the rest of their school day. Using yoga techniques and strategies in schools is becoming common and does not take long to implement. You will not be disappointed with the results!

Chapter 9: Differentiation in a Kids Yoga Class

Yoga can be incredibly beneficial for all children, but it has been found to be particularly true for kids with special needs. All of the benefits of yoga also directly tie in with the needs these children have. For example, motor skill development, building confidence, social skills, coping with stress, self-awareness, and sensory integration are skills that yoga incorporates. Numerous studies have also shown that yoga children with autism and Attention Deficit Hyperactivity Disorder (ADHD).

Yoga is effective for children with special needs because the class structure is consistent and routine. Every class begins with breathing and movement exercises. Concentration is improved as children try and learn new poses. Each class ends with a quiet time of Savasana, which the students look forward to. Children thrive on routine, and yoga is very consistent with this.

Yoga is very visual. Using visual tools such as the yoga pose cards (See Chapter 12) is helpful for working with different learners.

Kids are able to look at a yoga pose card and try to copy the posture even if they cannot verbalize what they are thinking. When kids see other kids doing yoga on the pose cards, they will want to try also.

Everyone learns differently, and yoga allows opportunities to meet students where they are. Every pose can be modified to give the feeling of success. Everything that children learn through yoga with poses, breathing exercises, relaxation techniques, and building self-awareness are all skills that can be used in their day-to-day lives.

Chapter 10: Using Yoga at Home With Your Kids

Doing yoga at home with your kids is a win-win situation for all. There are many benefits and advantages to introducing yoga to your children and it is easy to do. One advantage of yoga is that it can be done with kids of all ages. You can begin with simple poses with your kids as babies (or even while pregnant). Then continue on with preschoolers, school-age children, and through the teen years and beyond. This can be achieved by making some easy adaptations made as your children grow.

If you consistently make yoga a part of your life or even if you are brand new to yoga, you have probably already experienced, read, or heard about the definite benefits of yoga for all ages. Why wouldn't you want to introduce it to those you love most? Yoga provides many positives such as focus, mindfulness, stress reduction, flexibility, and physical strength, so it is understandable that you want to pass this practice on to your own children.

Connect With Your Child Through Yoga

Parents enjoy how yoga allows them to connect with their child. This can happen at any age and does not need to be in a formal yoga studio or classroom setting. This is something you can do *with* your children instead of being a spectator with activities such as soccer games, dance competitions, and piano recitals. I love cheering on my kids at their events and competitions, but it is a different memory when you do something *with* them.

Yoga helps you slow down and connect with your children—being in the moment, doing something together, and taking that experience with you. Yoga can be done anywhere. Take it outside, try it on the trampoline, or even in the rain. Just use your imagination. Laugh and have fun. Enthusiasm is contagious.

Keep It Simple

Introduce yoga poses that your child will be able to do. This will help build confidence and familiarity. Next move to other poses that are good for their bodies and minds. Keep in mind that children practicing poses will not look exactly like the pictures on the yoga cards or in magazines. Everyone's body is different and it is important to encourage your children to try their best, keep practicing, but most of all, have fun with it.

When my kids were younger, I was always looking for fun and active things we could do together. Yoga is a natural fit. Kids already love to move their bodies and are uninhibited to try new things. Yoga is a perfect way to burn off some energy when cooped up in the house during cold or rainy days. We would practice yoga poses on beach towels set up in our living room, played many rounds of Yoga Freeze Dance, and even kicked up into headstands and handstands against our living room wall.

Now that my children are out of the preschool years they love to actually practice a simple yoga flow with me. This is not something most children would request unless they've been exposed to yoga in some way beforehand. My oldest daughter comments that every time she finishes a yoga flow she cannot believe how "light she feels and clean inside."

Finding time to be active together as a family is hard with busy schedules and recurring commitments but yoga is something that does not need to take a lot of time. It is noncompetitive, has no cost involved, and all ages can enjoy together. This in turn makes it perfect for a family activity!

Simple Tips for Doing Yoga at Home With Your Kids

- **Make it Fun:** Don't take it too seriously. Children should feel like yoga is play and not work. Get down on the floor with them to play and practice poses. Be in the moment. They will love it! Kids yoga is very different from adult yoga so understand they will not have the same attention span. Follow *Go Go Yoga Kids* simple class outline in Chapter 2 and modify to suit you and your children's needs.

- **Keep it Simple:** It can be fun to use a theme and choose poses that correspond, but it is not required. Try to include some of the components of the class outline so your child can work on calming breath strategies and skills such as balance. A good rule of thumb is just begin by incorporating yoga in small ways throughout the day such as doing the same bed time calming stretches or morning wake up routine.

- **Use Props:** Grab some beach towels to lay out and sit on. Kids love having their own space and this will give them boundaries and a sense of ownership. Include your child's favorite stuffed animal and have it participate in balance exercises and snuggling for Savasana.

- **Partner Up:** There are many yoga poses that can be done with adults and children. Refer to the "Partner and Group Poses" in Chapter 3. Some of my favorite parent child poses are Partner Tree and See-Saw.

- **Pick a Card:** Utilizing yoga pose cards (found in Chapter 12) at home gives your kids the opportunity to choose poses they want to practice and provides a good visual reference. Let your child pick three to six yoga pose cards and practice them with the games and challenges found in Chapter 3.

- **Use a Story:** This is one of my favorite ways to practice yoga with kids. I love reading aloud to my kids and know how important it is to begin at an early age. They will receive the benefits of reading aloud AND practicing yoga. Animal stories tend to work well. When you get to a part about a particular animal such as a snake, cat, horse, or bug, pause to do the corresponding pose. *The Go Go Yoga Kids* resources in Chapter 12 includes many children's books that would work well for this.

Doing yoga at home doesn't need to be a fully structured class. During a stressful or frustrating time, remind your children to use their breath. Use the yoga breath ideas found in Chapter 3 for some great age-appropriate choices. Children will become more aware of their breath and the poses as they practice. Do not expect them to breathe deeply with focus on their first attempts. This will come as yoga is made part of a routine.

Have fun with yoga together! Make it a part of your life. There is no right or wrong way, but the fact that you are together, learning, and moving will create lasting memories with your children.

Chapter 11:
Creating Mindfulness in Kids

Being present and practicing mindfulness are words and concepts that are becoming more common in the media, among education leaders, and parents who want that for their children and themselves. There is something to be said for appreciating the moment you are in, but in our fast-paced society and lives, it is becoming increasingly difficult. With a few simple strategies and implementations in your day-to-day lives, it will become easier for you and the kids you care about.

We tell kids to pay attention all the time, but do they know how? Mindfulness is described as paying attention on purpose. We have been told practicing mindfulness is good for us. It is also great to teach our kids. There is significant research on how mindfulness can help children improve their attention span, calm down, reduce stress, regulate emotions, and encourage better memory and concentration.

We want to teach our children to develop their awareness so they can recognize when their attention has wandered, develop strategies for decreasing impulsive behavior, and learn how to calm the part of their brain that makes them upset. It is about getting children to reflect on their own thoughts and actions and to learn how to make better choices for themselves and others as well. This is a skill that is important to model and practice with children.

Being mindful sounds good, but it can be difficult to even get started let alone make it into a daily practice. Kids are busy. They have commitments from the moment they wake until bedtime and then into the weekend. No wonder it can be difficult for kids to just be. It is interesting to note how it doesn't start out like that for growing kids. Picture a preschooler noticing the shape of a leaf or the color of the sky as they dawdle along. Sadly, many kids slowly become accustomed to a hectic lifestyle, and they need to be reminded that it doesn't always need to be that way.

Practicing Mindfulness at Home

Parents often complain their children do not appreciate all that they have and constantly want the newest toy or latest gadget. We have to remember that kids are not born with a sense of gratitude. It is something that needs to be modeled and taught. One of the easiest (and best ways) to model mindfulness is to become mindful yourself.

Practice being in the moment with what you are doing whether on your own or with your kids. Pause and enjoy what you are doing *while* you are doing it. Only when we are truly present can we fully enjoy gratitude and be truly happy and content. Those are the moments that are remembered.

I know this sounds like easy advice, but when was the last time you really tried sitting, playing, and being engaged with that "Go Fish" game or something else that your child has been begging you to do with them? Did you do it without thinking of what else you should be doing—ie: laundry, dishes, phone calls to make? How often are you in one place doing one thing but thinking of something else? We know we do it, and we make repeated resolutions to "live in the now," but then life happens, and we find ourselves quickly reverting back to the same impulses and habits.

Make Mindfulness Part of a Routine

If you can commit to giving your full and undivided attention to the same two routines each day, you will slowly be able to add mindfulness to your day. This will help your children be more mindful. They are watching and modeling after you, it makes no difference their age. They are noticing.

Start small. Pick two times per day that you are really able to practice mindfulness. For example, an easy time for me to model and practice mindfulness is at the dinner table. That is when we all make a concentrated effort to gather together and eat as a family. The actual time we sit down for dinner varies wildly and will either take place before or after the evening activity whirlwind. The actual time does not make a difference. The point is being together, fully present, and focused on one another.

My mindful moment is during our bedtime routine. I make a concentrated effort to give each child one-on-one time and try to keep the "reminders about tomorrow" and "homework completion" questions to a minimum. For 5-15 minutes of one-on-one time I am fully present. Our best discussions often take place when they are settled in for the night, their bodies slowing down, and their hearts open.

Your designated mindful moments may be different. Maybe it's your commute to or from work. Turn the music off, mute the cell phone, and do nothing (except drive mindfully). Pay attention to the sights and sounds around you.

Some people find great success meditating first thing in the morning or during yoga and exercise time each day. Think of something that you do each day and make a commitment to being fully present and engaged with whatever it is. I walk my youngest child to the bus each morning. It is a short walk down the street, but during that time, I am all about the moment. During that time I am fully present. It is one of my favorite parts of the day.

Mindfulness Methods to Use With Kids

- **Validate Their Feelings**: Many times we tell kids "You're fine," or "It's not a big deal." However, it is a big deal to children who live in the present moment. Help them recognize their emotions—sadness, fear, worry, frustration—and let them know it is okay to feel that way. Once they see that they are understood, then you can work on helping them manage those emotions in a mindful way.
- **Introduce Mindful Breathing:** We talk a lot about the importance of Breath Work in Chapter 3. Teaching children to become aware of their breath does not need to be a structured

activity. Simply have the children sit comfortably and close their eyes. Have them bring their attention to their breath, which means noticing the sensation of breath coming in and going out of their bodies. The kids can place their hands on their stomachs to feel the rise and fall of each breath.

One of my favorite breath techniques to teach kids is the Five Finger Breath. This easy Breath Work exercise can be done anywhere to help bring about calmness, reduce anxiety, or just re-center and transition from a highly stimulated event to a quieter and more focused time. Begin with gently closed fists. With each exhale, uncurl a finger from your fist. Pause and inhale. On your next exhale, uncurl another finger. Continue until both of your palms are open. The Five Finger Breath is especially wonderful for children who get over stimulated easily or have special needs.

- **Turn on All 5 Senses:** This can be made into a game, not just a "mindful exercise." I practiced this recently with my son by going on a mindful walk. We had talked about our five senses and how we were going to utilize them all (except taste) on our walk in the woods while waiting for his sister's soccer game to start. For 60 seconds we walked in complete silence. After a minute passed, we talked about the things we had noticed and heard. Max and I had completely different things to share from what we had just experienced—on the same walk. Turning on your senses can be done anywhere: the grocery store, the donut shop, the mall, and especially when you are outdoors. It doesn't take long and can make whatever you are doing or where you are more mindful and memorable.
- **Pick a Sense, Any Sense:** This can be done by giving kids an object—rock, feather, fabric, squishy ball, rain stick, bell—and then have them describe it in words that pertain to the one sense you are focusing on. Examples: How does the feather feel or what does the squishy ball sound like when you squeeze it?

- **This is My Heartbeat Song:** Have the children do various exercises to get their heart rates up and pumping. After one minute of activity, have them stop and place their hands on their hearts. What do they feel? What do they notice about their breath and their bodies?
- **Have a Mantra:** This technique is helpful to use when in a difficult or stressful situation. When I first tried meditating it was impossible for me to clear my head and achieve a "blank slate" in my mind. Thoughts kept drifting in and out one right after the other. I called it my monkey mind, meaning it was busy but not accomplishing much. A yoga instructor suggested trying a mantra during my meditation time, and that worked perfectly for me. Instead of focusing on *not thinking,* I instead could repeat my mantra over and over and found it very calming and meditative.

Mantras can easily be taught to kids. Make them simple and easy to remember, which is then wonderful for them to use in a stressful moment or a time of unease. Effective mantras for kids could be: "I am thankful," "I am loved," "I am safe," or "Let it go," which is also a great one for adults.

- **Practice Mindful Eating:** This strategy would go along perfectly with mindful dinner times with your family. Try to remember the last time you really paid attention to all of the sights, smells, textures, and tastes of your food. Start by chewing each bite thoroughly for 20-30 seconds and truly enjoying what you are experiencing. Let your children know that you are grateful for what you are eating and who you are spending your time with.

Another fun way to practice mindfulness with eating and with kids is to give each of them a small piece of chocolate or sweet treat. Delay gratification by making them wait and appreciate before eating it. When they do finally take a bite, ask them to truly notice, savor, and appreciate this tiny morsel as they eat it very slowly.

- **Squeeze and Relax:** Kids enjoy doing this exercise and don't even realize it is a meditation. It is perfect to do before bedtime and settling in for the night, and it works well in schools before a test or another stressful situation. If kids are lying down or sitting in a chair, have them tighten every muscle in their bodies.  They can squeeze their legs, arms, fists, and close their eyes tightly. Have them hold this position for a few moments and then release and relax. Ask them how their bodies feel different. This fun activity helps to make kids fully present as you feel all of your muscles tensing and relaxing.

- **Give Thanks:** This can be done anywhere and in a variety of ways. It works for our family at the dinner table as we share what we are thankful or grateful for in our day. Gratitude journals are also wonderful to use with adults and kids. These journals do not need to be a long narrative each day about all of your blessings, but instead can be a few written lines. I have had fun using hashtags in my gratitude journal. I like those because they are simple, easy, and to the point. I might have gotten that idea from my hashtag-loving teenage daughter.

- **Catch Them Being Good:** This one truly works on all ages of kids. I use it on my kids at home and my students at school. Which technique will provide a better response, constantly pointing out what they are doing wrong or praising them for making correct choices? Everyone loves to receive recognition and praise for a job well done, being mindful, and behaving well. I especially like to use this strategy with my "spirited" students since they often receive negative comments or redirection. Receiving praise greatly increases the likelihood they will choose that behavior again, which decreases the negative behavior. Over time they may begin to recognize and appreciate others around them.

- **Keep it Short:** Mindfulness moments are not about who can be mindful the longest. It is definitely a quality over quantity practice. It is best when it is kept to five minutes or less and to truly be in the moment. With regular practice, you will find kids getting better at the techniques and using them on their own.

- **Find a Good Kids Yoga Class:** A quality class can provide wonderful opportunities for kids to practice mindfulness on their own and with others. Students begin by settling into the moment and focusing on their breath and body. Next, they practice engaging poses with games that focus on cooperation and teamwork. Class ends with Savasana or quiet time. The end of class usually becomes the students' favorite part while they lie still and "do nothing," which is mindfulness in its own way. Students know they worked their bodies hard, and this is a time to give back, be still, and reap the benefits of strengthening their bodies and minds. Being involved in a quality yoga class keeps the kids present, aware, and in the moment, which is a valuable skill to practice throughout life.

Try incorporating some of these mindful strategies in your day-to-day life for yourself and with your children. It doesn't take much time, but let the contentment, focus, and appreciation for these moments envelop your lives, and know that it's worth it.

Chapter 12: Yoga for Kids Resources

Books to Use For Kids Yoga

Using picture books in my yoga classes helps tie together yoga poses and themes, while reading aloud to kids while incorporating yoga helps them be fit and literate. I have found the illustrations help children visualize or pretend to become that animal or feel as if they are in the story. When you add movement, the kids will remember the poses and the story even more as they anticipate what comes next.

Many children's books work well, and you probably have a few favorites of your own. The important thing to remember is to let the book come alive by reading with enthusiasm and emotion. Make your yoga poses simple or complex depending on the story line.

A lot of picture books can be used with different yoga themes. For example, *The Very Hungry Caterpillar* by Eric Carle is wonderful to use in learning about spring transformations in nature. It is fun to act out since kids can transition through the different stages of becoming a butterfly. See the Spring Themed Yoga Lesson Plan in Chapter 4 for additional suggestions on this fun idea.

Below are some books I've had great success with;

Animal Themed Books

The following books are fun to use with ages 3-9. They include animals that can easily correspond with a yoga pose. When a new animal is introduced in the story, pause and show the kids a yoga pose that would relate to that animal. These books are especially wonderful for those children who are kinesthetic learners since they often need to be moving while learning.

- *If You Give a Mouse a Cookie* by Laura Joffe Numeroff can be used to introduce mouse and snake poses.
- *Duck on a Bike* by David Shannon is another favorite. It involves fun opportunities for animal poses and kids can relate to learning how to ride a bike.
- *Lion and the Mouse* by Jerry Pinkney is perfect for lion and mouse poses.
- *Ten Monkey Jamboree* by Dianne Ochiltree is a good choice for Monkey Pose.
- *Bear's New Friend* by Karma Wilson is fun for practicing Owl Pose. Roll up your yoga mat and perch upon it as if you are an owl. Kids absolutely love doing this.
- *Pete the Cat* by Eric Litwin can be used to practice Cat Pose. Its catchy words will definitely have kids moving.
- *I Want My Hat Back* by Jon Klassen is an award-winning fun story that features a bear and other animals.
- *The Pigeon Finds a Hot Dog* by Mo Willems is fun to listen to and then to practice Pigeon Pose.
- *The Very Bad Bunny* by Marilyn Sadler is a great choice for Bunny Pose or any springtime theme.
- *Mouse Count* by Ellen Walsh can be used to introduce the concept of being "quiet as a mouse" for Savasana. You can also practice mouse and snake poses with this book.
- *Brown Bear, Brown Bear, What Do You See?* by Bill Martin Jr. includes many wonderful animal poses. Please refer to the Brown Bear Lesson Plan in Chapter 4 for many ideas on using this book.
- *Dinosaurs Galore* by Giles Andreae: Please refer to the Dinosaur Themed Parent Note in Chapter 10 for ideas.

Nature and Seasonal Themed Books

These books are fun to read when the weather is starting to change outside or just before holidays. Children are naturally excited around seasonal changes and holidays and these books and related poses will help them anticipate and appreciate the season even more.

- *The Very Hungry Caterpillar* by Eric Carle is perfect for caterpillar, cocoon, and butterfly poses. Please refer to the Spring Time lesson plan in Chapter 4.
- *Rumble in the Jungle* by Giles Andreae and David Wojtowycz can be used with the Welcome to the Jungle lesson plan in Chapter 4 or used itself for practicing animal poses.
- *Earth Dance* by Joanne Ryder is a wonderful book for celebrating Earth Day every day and can involve a lot of movement.
- *Muncha! Muncha! Muncha!* by Candace Fleming is a great choice for a spring time/growing things theme (Chapter 4) or practicing Bunny Pose.
- *The Tiny Seed* by Eric Carle can be used for a seed to flower theme. Please refer to Chapter 4.
- *The Little Old Lady Who Wasn't Afraid of Anything* by Linda Williams is a fun and easy read to use with the fall theme in the lesson plans, and it also involves a lot of movement.

Feelings Themed Books

Yoga is about recognizing and managing your own feelings as well as developing empathy and kindness toward others. Reading these books aloud will open up the door for conversations about how we feel on the inside and how we treat others.

- *My Many Colored Days* by Eric Carle is a great book for recognizing different emotions and self-awareness. Older children enjoy this book as well.
- *The Giving Tree* by Shel Silverstein is a classic favorite that can be used to discuss friendship, empathy, and even some Tree Pose practice!
- *The Pout-Pout Fish in the Big-Big Dark* by Deborah Diesen has themes of friendship and overcoming fears as well a catchy refrain.
- *You Will Be My Friend* by Peter Brown is a fun story that has several animals for yoga poses but also includes a wonderful message on friendship.

- *The Rainbow Fish* by Marcus Pfister can be used to talk about friendship and to practice Fish Pose.
- *Swimmy* by Leo Lionni is a favorite book for learning about working together and cooperation.
- *Little Quack* by Lauren Thompson has a lot of teachable components, including overcoming fears, encouraging one another, and practicing Duck Pose.
- *The Museum* by Susan Verde is a beautifully illustrated book that showcases the importance of being yourself while inspiring creativity.

Fun Themed Related Books

Children will learn and gain something from all read alouds, but these books were specifically chosen for the learning aspect. The following books are wonderful to use in a school, studio, or home setting.

- *Commotion in the Ocean* by Giles Andreae and David Wojtowycz is a perfect book for learning about different ocean animals. Refer to the Ocean Themed lesson plans in Chapter 4 for more ideas.
- *Chicka Chicka Boom Boom* by Bill Martin, Jr. is a great choice for younger ages during an alphabet themed class and for practicing Tree Pose.
- *King Bidgood's in the Bathtub* by Audrey and Don Wood is a favorite to use for the medieval times theme found in Chapter 4.
- *Eliot Jones, Midnight Superhero* by Anne Cottringer has a great tie in for the Superheroes Lesson in Chapter 4.

Active Movement Related Books

These books are wonderful to get kids up and moving while reading aloud.

- *From Head to Toe* by Eric Carle can be used for Active Movement at the beginning of a yoga class and at home to help kids become aware of their bodies.

- *Where the Wild Things Are* by Maurice Sendak is fun to get kids moving while you have your own wild rumpus dance party.
- *How Can You Dance?* by Rick Walton is a fun book choice to get everyone up and dancing.
- *I am Yoga* by Susan Verde is a beautifully written and illustrated book that can be used to learn and explore many different yoga poses.

Books to Read Aloud at Home

In my opinion, there is no better way to spend quality time with your children than snuggling up and reading aloud. I am always on the lookout for quality books that I know children will enjoy. The following books are specifically written for special moments with your kids when they (and you) will learn and experience something new … together.

- *Extra Yarn* by Mac Barnett and Jon Klassen is a sweet Caldecott Honor book about making an impact on the world, one small piece at a time.
- *Koala Lou* by Mem Fox is a favorite among parents and kids and is a story about unconditional love.
- *Good Night Yoga* and *Good Morning Yoga* are by one of my favorite children authors, Mariam Gates. These books provide the perfect evening or morning routines for kids that help them begin and end their day with positivity and confidence.
- *A Handful of Quiet: Happiness in Four Pebbles* by Thich Nhat Hanh is an insightful and hands-on approach to bring meditation to life using four ordinary pebbles in a way that kids will be able to relate to.
- *The Runaway Bunny* by Margaret Wise Brown tells the story of love between child and parent.
- *Goodnight Moon* by Margaret Wise Brown is a memorable, classic night-time story for kids.

Music For Kids Yoga

Kids naturally want to move to music and having a variety of songs helps keep kids engaged. I like to use music during the Active Movement, Games, and Savasana portions of class (Chapter 3), but it can be incorporated any place you see fit.

Here are some examples of music I have used with kids:

Ages 3-6

- Justin Roberts (Great Big Sun is perfect for Sun Salutations)
- Any Disney soundtrack
- Raffi
- Tumble Tots
- Bingo Kids
- Putumayo African Playground
- Kira Willey (Dance for the Sun)
- The Laurie Berkner Band
- The Wiggles (Shake Your Sillies Out)
- Greg & Steve (The Freeze)
- Israel "Iz" Kamakawiwo'ole (Somewhere Over the Rainbow). This song is a great choice for Savasana as you can place a "rainbow" over the kids from head to feet as they are lying down.

Ages 7-11

This age group enjoys current pop artists such as Taylor Swift, MC Yogi (Give Love), Ingrid Michaelson, Michael Franti, and Spearhead. I also use music from Kids Bop or find additional playlists on Pandora or Spotify.

There are people gifted at making playlists for kids yoga and make them available online. Take advantage of these resources, especially in the beginning as you find out what works for you and what doesn't. Your students will develop favorites and familiarity, and that is a good thing.

Yoga Resources

Yoga Pose Cards

Yoga Pretzels (Yoga Cards) 50 Fun Yoga Activities for Kids and Grownups by Tara Guber and Leah Kalish

These are my favorite pose cards and I use them nearly every class. These illustrated cards include balance, partner work, and relaxation poses. The back of the cards include kid friendly directions on how to practice the poses.

Web Links

A list of additional kids yoga resources are located at GoGoYogaKids.com

About the Author

Kids, yoga, and teaching are truly Sara Weis' passions. When the idea for *Go Go Yoga Kids: Empower Kids For Life Through Yoga* came to Sara, she knew it was the perfect way to share her excitement and strong belief in the positive power of yoga with others.

"Introducing kids to the lifelong benefits of yoga in fun, creative, and engaging ways is something I feel very passionate about," said Sara. "It is my hope that anyone who has kids or works with kids will be able to use *Go Go Yoga Kids* with confidence and success. The benefits kids receive from yoga are too important to miss. Now is the perfect time to start using yoga to empower kids for life!"

Sara is a certified kid and adult yoga instructor who makes yoga with kids or adults part of her daily routine. She has invested countless hours creating and leading yoga games, lessons, and movement ideas with thousands of kids. Over the years she has learned what works, and just as importantly, what doesn't work with kids and yoga. "I feel strongly about my goal of having all of the ideas, strategies, and lessons in one place so this book can be a complete resource for others to use when introducing yoga to kids," she said.

Sara holds a master's degree in Education and has over seventeen years of teaching experience in the public schools. She currently teaches creative writing classes for elementary and junior high aged students. Sara also leads kids yoga classes for a nationally known health and fitness club.

When she is not teaching, writing, or practicing yoga, Sara enjoys spending time outdoors with her three yogi kids and her husband and resides in West Des Moines, Iowa.

Connect with Go Go Yoga Kids!

🌐	www.gogoyogakids.com
f	www.facebook.com/GoGoYogaKids
🐦	www.twitter.com/GoGoYogaKids
📷	www.instagram.com/GoGoYogaKids
📌	www.pinterest.com/GoGoYogaKids

Index

JUN 0 9 2017

CPSIA information can be obtained
at www.ICGtesting.com
Printed in the USA
LVOW03s1625140417
530760LV00003B/30/P